Like Water or Clouds

The T'ang Dynasty and the Tao

A. S. Kline

POETRY IN TRANSLATION

www.poetryintranslation.com

Please direct sales or editorial enquiries to:
tonykline@poetryintranslation.com

This print edition is published by
Poetry In Translation (*www.poetryintranslation.com*),
via On-Demand Publishing LLC, (a Delaware limited liability Company that does business under the name "CreateSpace") in partnership with
Amazon EU S.à.r.l. (a Luxembourg company with registration number B-101818 and its registered office at 5 Rue Plaetis, L-2338, Luxembourg)

ISBN-10: 1505685524
ISBN-13: 978-1505685527

✒ Contents ✒

➤ AUTHOR'S NOTE ☚

There is a problem for the reader of books about China and the Chinese, or of Chinese poems in translation, due to the variation in spelling of Chinese names and terms. This is caused by the many systems of transliteration used in the past when rendering Chinese names into English. It may make it difficult for the reader who knows no Chinese to recognise the same person place or term in different guises.

Modern China uses the Pinyin system (e.g. Beijing for Peking) for Romanization of names, which is still unfamiliar and awkward for most readers in the West who are used to the older systems.

I have therefore used traditional spellings in this book so that readers can recognise the names when referring to the many translations of Chinese poetry that already exist in English, and to older historical and biographical texts.

However readers wanting to refer to modern Atlases of China, for place names, or to other modern texts, will find a comprehensive list of equivalent names and terms towards the end of the book. This includes a Pinyin spelling for each name or term and for place-names the modern province name to assist when referring to an Atlas.

THE T'ANG DYNASTY AND THE TAO

Fishing Village in Moonlight, Gu Liang (15th century)

The Way - cannot be told.
The Name - cannot be named.
The nameless is the Way of Heaven and Earth.
The named is Matrix of the Myriad Creatures.
Eliminate desire to find the Way.
Embrace desire to know the Creature.

The Tao Te Ching I

Exhibit the unadorned.
Hold fast to the un-carved block.
Avoid the thought of Self.
Eliminate desire.

The Tao Te Ching XIX

The Way has no name.
The un-carved block is small
But no one dare claim it.
When it is carved there are names.
When there are names it is time to stop.

The Tao Te Ching XXXII

INTRODUCTION

The West is a sharpened blade. Western reason and Science have had as their goal the precise and the definitive, the form without shadow, the known and the named. The Classical aspiration was to describe and to understand, to define and to capture. The aspirations of the East were different.

Mathematics is the primary language by which the West has attempted to describe the approximate and imprecise. The formula encapsulates theory. What cannot be visualised can still be predicted with high degrees of accuracy. The predictability of outcomes and the consistency of experimental results are the core of science. The predictive capability of science is the platform for technology.

The East took an alternative path. Ancient India and China accepted the primacy of the unnameable, the imprecise, the evanescent, and the indistinct. The essences of Taoism and Buddhism are the Vortex and the Void, respectively, that which cannot be captured, and that which cannot be described, the nameless and the featureless.

Eastern religion has strongly influenced Western religion and art, but the direction that Western society has taken has been towards exact definition framed in secular language. Society has been defined by the search for a coherent legal system, and Science by the search for truth embodied in exact descriptions and universal laws. Of the ways of thought in China, Taoism in particular has prized instead the evanescent and rarified, the vacant and turbid, the indistinct and shadowy, the tentative and hesitant.

It is true that the West has valued these aspects of thought in art. In painting for example there is the light and shadow effect of *chiarascuro* in Leonardo Da Vinci's and Rembrandt's work. It has valued them in music in the tonal subtleties of Beethoven's last quartets, or Brahms's and Chopin's solo piano pieces. It has valued them in the troubled existentialist thinking of a Kierkegaard, the mysticism of a St John of the Cross, the quietism of certain poets. It has valued, in all the arts, moments of introspection and stillness. But insight in the West has more often meant instances of revelation than consistent durable attitude. Apollo and Dionysus have been the patrons of the arts. Apollo is the god of clear form, intense light and the bounding line. Dionysus is the god of intense energy, ecstasy and the reforming chaos. One has been the patron of Classical order and moderation, the other the patron of turbulence and Revolution. Both are fundamentally masculine, neither are quietist. Western art, religion and philosophy have tended to espouse the directed, the purposeful, the charged, and the dynamic. The quiet contemplatives are an exception rather than a rule. They have rarely generated schools of thought. They have been isolated examples.

Ancient China on the other hand valued the feminine, and attempted to keep the masculine in balance, to mute it and subdue it, to restrain it and absorb it. Quietism is a marked feature of Taoism the fundamental thought pattern of ancient China, and also of Chinese Buddhism and Confucianism the other two great ethical movements. Each of the three differs in its solutions. Simplistically Buddhism is a transcending of the world of transient phenomena: Confucianism is a continuing engagement with the world in its social aspects: while Taoism is an acceptance of and conformance with the world's fundamental natural energies. Nevertheless there is a common underlying approach, a search for a self-illuminating harmony that is intrinsically personal, modest and moderate.

By the time of the T'ang Dynasty in the eighth century AD Taoist and Buddhist thought was well over a thousand years old. Buddhism imported from India was established in China by 65 AD and found in Taoism a natural forerunner. In their original forms neither way of thought is a religion in the Western sense. There are no gods, personal or otherwise. There is no sentience in the universe. There is no ostensible pre-determined purpose for existence. Human beings in Buddhist thinking are potentially caught up on an endless wheel of rebirth and the goal is an individual one, to find a way of casting off the pain and constraints of life, to achieve personal freedom and enlightenment. The Buddhist goal is the Void, *nirvana,* where the Self vanishes. The Taoist goal is to be part of the flow of universal energies, *the Tao,* that Vortex which is in its totality aimless and directionless.

Taoism, Buddhism and Confucianism were the intellectual matrix of the T'ang period. Fully developed approaches to the problems of existence, as they were, they informed and illuminated the lives of the T'ang poets and painters. It was in poetry, in the works of three major poets in particular, Li Po (pronounced in modern Chinese as if it were spelt Lee Baw, the first name in China being the surname), Wang Wei (Wang Way), and Tu Fu (Doo Foo) that the T'ang Dynasty achieved its greatest artistic flowering. Wang Wei was also a famous painter, and part of the line of development that led to the high achievements of later Chinese landscape painting imbued with the spirit of Taoism.

The lives of these three men began in the relative peace and stability of the T'ang Dynasty with its centralised Imperial government based on the Court of the Emperor and his ministers, wives and concubines. China's Imperial history, before and since, was turbulent and often unstable though the thread of centralised Imperial rule ran through it, and the ethical systems and social rituals provided fundamental continuities.

The three poets were born within a few years of each other around the start of the eighth century AD. Wang Wei in 699AD, Li Po in 701 and Tu Fu, the youngest of the three, in 712. The T'ang Dynasty had achieved a period of calm and consolidation. The majority of their adult years were lived in the reign of Hsüan-tsung who ruled from 712 to 756AD. Known as Ming-huang the Glorious Monarch, Hsüan-tsung was a patron of poetry music and the arts. He was also a scholar of Taoism and Esoteric Buddhism. Under his reformed administration Chinese civilisation flowered. The borders of the immense Empire were garrisoned and defended, allowing almost fifty years of uninterrupted splendour. However his infatuation with a concubine Yang Kuei-fei led inexorably to the disaster of the An Lu-shan rebellion. In 756 the Emperor fled south-west to Szechwan and the period of greatness was over.

Wang Wei, Li Po and Tu Fu lived through the time of civil war, destruction and tragedy. Wang died in 759, Hsüan-tsung himself in 761, Li in 762 and Tu in 770AD, so that despite the later re-instatement of the T'ang Dynasty, their lives broadly coincide with the flowering and fading of this period of cultural magnificence. The rebellion of General An Lu-shan was a further example of the many episodes of war and violence that punctuated Chinese Imperial history. It dismayed those with leanings to Confucianism, and confirmed for the Taoists and Buddhists the wisdom of retreat from a world of turmoil and confusion.

The lives and art of the three poets illustrate the tensions between involvement and non-involvement. Their poetry is full of humanity, delight in the natural world, and celebration of the everyday that enables it still to communicate with us across the centuries. But it is also filled with aspiration towards the greater life through Confucian integrity, Taoist retreat and Buddhist non-attachment. Through it run positive feelings of affection, friendship, and appreciation of beauty and tranquillity. But there is also sadness at transience, regret for what is lost, pathos, and compassion.

Each is highly individual but all three reveal their empathy, sensitivity and sincerity. They struggled with the demands of their society and also the needs of their own psyches. They aspired to peace and inner calm but found themselves also engaged in a difficult world. Nothing is easy for those who wish to live the better life. It was not straightforward for these men in the ancient East any more than for us in the modern West. Certainly there was both a high moral and mental challenge, demanding intellectual, emotional and ethical responsiveness. Confucianism requires engagement. Taoism and Buddhism are not simple escapes from reality. They require a profound change in mental attitude.

Resistance to the concepts of both the void and the vortex is immense in the West. One seems merely emptiness, the other chaos. Our culture has led us into different channels. All our instincts are towards form and order, purpose and direction, achievement and activity. We introspect endlessly but we find contemplation difficult. We are fascinated by Leonardo's drawings of water or Rembrandt's figures lost in personal meditation. But they are exceptions within the mainstream of our culture. In literature for example there are few examples of the vortex or the contemplation of the void. Dante, Tolstoy, Shakespeare, Goethe are miracles of substantial, positive, directed energy. Dante's contemplation of the afterlife resembles a set of scientific observations. Tolstoy's and Shakespeare's characters are carved out of the air with that precision we also admire in Jane Austen, and with the fecundity of creation we admire in Dickens. Homer, Sophocles, Ovid, Petrarch, Racine, Pushkin set the Western tone of clarity, brilliance, delineation, and externality. Inwardness and introspection are less evident in poetry than we might think. Quietism is rare in all the western arts. The best examples are in piano and chamber music and landscape painting, in the silence and stillness of the canvas, and the complex, muted tonalities and intimate harmonies of stringed instruments. Apollo and Dionysus are more often present in them. The void and the vortex rarely. We are able to enter Chinese art, particularly T'ang poetry and Sung painting, through an appreciation of natural beauty, but it can often seem understated, simplistic, muted and casual to the Western mind.

Buddhist, Confucian and Taoist ways of thought are each different. However Taoist spontaneity and sensitivity underlies the creation of almost all of Classical China's poetry, painting and three-dimensional objects. The common artistic inheritance, the means of expression, and the Imperial culture blended together the three streams of thought, with the underlying Taoist concepts ever present. They are concepts that differ fundamentally from the traditional concepts of the West. Modern China as it follows Western capitalism and technology will find itself increasingly at odds with its own cultural history. The Western mind would itself need a radical change of its fundamental thought processes in order to approach the Tao. Taoism is spontaneous, non-intrusive, quiescent, empty, inactive and indifferent. It is the opposite of a scientific discipline, even though certain of its subordinate esoteric practises stimulated early technologies in China. Its essence is *wu-wei* the principle of non-action. Its goal is not achievable by the will. Its teachings cannot be communicated in words. It claims nothing and demands nothing.

The history of China, the lives of the poets and painters all demonstrate the difficulty of living in the world and aspiring to reach the Tao. The Chinese were as human and as fallible as we are. The true Taoist adept almost by definition is not a committed poet or painter, and cannot play a key role in the social order. The adept is not engaged with the world in that way. Taoism in the arts is almost a leakage from the pure Way into the impure human world. The Tao remains often only an aspiration and thereby an inspiration. The achievements of T'ang poetry are inevitably bound up with the external society, with the fate of the Dynasty and the lives of the poets. Wang Wei is an example of the modest official finding his solace in retreat to his country estate, in the practise of art, and in the study of Buddhist texts. Tu Fu is the humane Confucian, trying to be of service, demanding moral integrity of himself and of others, accepting with sadness the vagaries of fate, exploiting the absorbing technical possibilities of poetry. Li Po is the Romantic, otherworldly, careless genius who scatters brilliance, dreams of a reality beyond the real, and exemplifies the spontaneity and grace of the Taoist Way. Their lives are illuminated by the transient splendour of the T'ang zenith, and then darkened by the shadow of its fall. Regret, nostalgia for the vanished glories, memory of past joys, the horrors of war, the pain of shifting allegiance, the hurt of separation from those loved, the effects of time and of distance, of ageing and of loss, are all present in their poetry.

But equally present are other factors, strength of character, deep sensibility, love of nature, pity and compassion, friendship and tenderness, which emphasise the ability of the poets to see all life and see it whole. Pity is not self-pity. The indifference of nature is not evidence of its active hostility. The lack of external purpose is not a reason for lack of internal knowledge of the right goals of living. Misfortune is not a justification for narrowness or lack of tenderness. Separation enhances friendship and love. Poetry and the arts, beauty and grace shed light on life.

There are trios of related elements. There are the three poets, Wang Wei, Li Po and Tu Fu. There are the three attitudes to existence, the three ways of life, of Buddhism, Taoism and Confucianism. There are the three main protagonists of the Imperial tragedy, Hsüan-tsung the Emperor, Yang Kuei-fei the beloved concubine and consort, and An Lu-Shan the rebellious general. There are the three key aspects of life, the social, spiritual and artistic. It is through these triplicities we can attempt to see into the past.

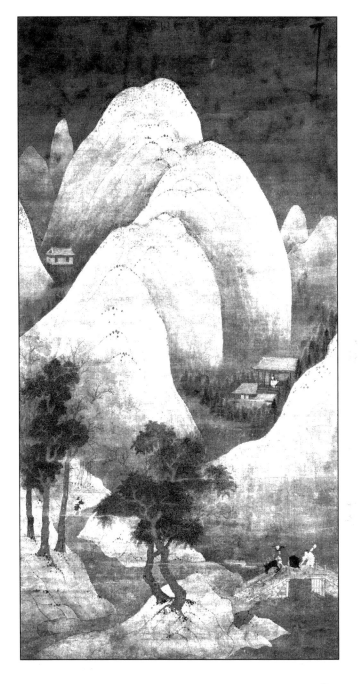

Clearing after Snow in Streams and Mountains, Yang Sheng (17th century)

THE TAO

The Tao is the Vortex. The way to it lies in the recognition of the fluidity and instability of the Universe. Its deepest nature is like water or clouds. Nevertheless it encompasses the emergence of all forms. It underlies the Yang elements of existence, brightness, strength, and precise form, heat and light, jade and mountain, phoenix and dragon. Yet it is also the Yin matrix the female spirit of the valley, moon and shadow, winter and the north, mists and rivers, the containing cave and the opening flower.

The Vortex is the movement of energies and the energies themselves. It is that seething world of sub-atomic entities that the quantum universe displays and it is the structures of the macrocosm. It is both form and chaos. At its core are randomness and uncertainty. It is chaotic like the atmosphere, like the waterfall, but it reveals continuously altering form like the cloud and the river. From its inwardness come the myriad entities. Its surface ripples and undulates. Its depths twist and coil. It is eternal and continuous. It contains infinitely nested repetitive patterns, but never repeats itself in entirety. It changes and flows through time. Its changes *are* Time. Each reconfiguration of the Universe is the Moment. Bodies alter imperceptibly. Mountains erode. Rivers alter their course. Clouds rise and vanish.

The Tao is process, as our minds are. It is the movement of water in the mountain stream. It is the windblown cloud pouring across the dome of the sky. It is the cycle of individual birth, unique maturity and unknowable death within the pattern of the species and the type. It is the irregularity, the randomness that guarantees identity, and the form and process that reveals similarity. Thinking about the Tao breaks down our view of fixed boundaries, containing shapes, and permanent entities. It introduces the random fluctuation, the imageless particle and invisible wave. The static vibrates. The isolated merges. The world is an instant, an instance of the World.

The endlessly pouring, continuously flowing, imperceptibly altering, randomly changing, richly patterned universe of the myriad creatures emerges from the seething continuum that is the un-carved block. The un-carved block is both vast and minute, macrocosm and microcosm. It cannot be grasped in its smallness and cannot be grasped in its enormity. It is the unnamed and unnameable matrix in which all names are dissolved, but out of which all nameable things come. It is the great calmly moving ocean of forms, of earths, seas, skies and stars, that also reveals itself in the unstable, shifting, elusive and transient. It is the smoke patterns in the air, the currents of the river, the flickering of light, the fluctuations of lives. Energy flows through all forms, at many levels, in veins or threads. It makes the 'dragon veins' of landscapes employed in geomancy (*Feng shui*, 'wind and water'). It creates the texture of silk, the structure of a leaf or a flower, the elements of a thought. These veins and threads are part of the nature of a thing and the essence of a process. They are like the Tao indefinite and elusive, vague and slippery, subtle and hidden. But they may also like the Tao be simple and undemanding, various and gleaming, satisfying and clear.

The aim of Taoism is to reach a harmony with this matrix, with the Tao. Its goal is to be a tranquil part of the Vortex, to live among the currents and inner vortices. The Way is to hold to the uncarved block, the universal mystery, without the urge to name and analyse, classify and dissect. It is to embrace time and change, to recognise the continuum, to cease grasping, to suppress the will, to harmonise the energies, to let go of worldly objectives. That is why the Way is straightforward but intensely difficult. That is why it cannot be reached by an act of reason but is in itself wholly reasonable. Lao Tzu the author to whom the Tao Te Ching, the great classic of Taoism, is attributed says 'My words are simple and easy to use, but no one understands them or uses them.' 'The Way is straightforward but people prefer side tracks.' And of the nature of the Tao and therefore of the Universe itself he says, 'Without possession, without demands, without authority it is mysterious virtue.'

A Fisherman in a Landscape, Gao Qifeng (1889 – 1933)

EARLY CHINESE HISTORY

Taoism, Buddhism and Confucianism were ancient ways of thought long before the T'ang Dynasty. The Chinese civilisation itself was already more than two thousand years old when the T'ang Dynasty came to power. By 5000BC Neolithic peoples were cultivating the yellow loess soils of northern China, fine fertile, wind-driven and river-borne, soils workable with primitive tools. The soil is *huang tu*, yellow earth, ground to fine powder by the Arctic winds, and blown down from the Siberian Steppes. Loess has little structural stability and is carved into cliffs and gullies by rain, wind and rivers. The Chinese became skilled at hydraulic engineering on this immensely cultivable soil.

By 1500BC a sophisticated bronze-age civilisation, the Shang Dynasty, ruled in areas of the Yellow River valley and as far south as the Yangtze River. Around 1050BC the Shang was defeated in battle by King Wu and the Chou Dynasty was founded. From this period to 221BC a complex civilisation developed, consolidating fifty states through warfare, to bring the whole of the Yellow River plain under Chou control. The Chou period was decentralised, with frequent periods of political fragmentation, but contains the intellectual origins of Chinese thought. From this period come the earliest Chinese poetry, the Book of Songs, and the compilation of the Classic historical and ritual texts.

Confucianism dates from around 500BC. Confucius promoted the concept of an ordered social structure governed by morally based conventions and rituals. The highest virtue is *ren,* the life of benevolence, humanity, and conscience. Taoism also probably dates from this period, its oldest text, the Tao Te Ching of the possibly mythical teacher Lao Tzu, establishing its concept of the Way, the matrix of energy underlying the vortex of the natural world, and the life that is lived in harmony with the flows of existence.

The Ch'in Dynasty, which in turn in 206BC gave way to the great Han, was established about 250BC and by 221BC the Ch'in had consolidated the Empire to rule all of China. With Capitals at Ch'ang-an (modern Xian) and

Loyang, in Central China, the Empire stretched from Korea and Vietnam in the southeast to Central Asia in the northwest. From this period dates the terracotta army at Xian, found in the vicinity of the tomb of the First Ch'in Emperor. Ch'in built the first Great Wall that the Han used as an effective military barrier against border incursions.

Through military strength, taxation, legal decree, and cultural unity the Han Emperors established the strong central government that characterised later China. They extended trade routes across Asia to Persia, India, Arabia and Rome. The unified regime, based on an educated elite, Confucian in spirit with a Taoist admixture, encouraged art and the civilised life. Bronze and lacquer work produced was of rare beauty. Calligraphy flourished furthering the copying and study of the Five Classics, and ceramic production was advanced. This basically agrarian society, with its emphasis on family, filial piety, the subservience of women, Confucian-educated officials, strong central Imperial control, defended borders, and a common moral and legal cultural framework set the pattern for later Dynasties.

The luxury of the Imperial Court, the presence of Imperial concubines and eunuchs, and the principle of exogamy, that is the requirement of the Emperors to marry a subject outside the line of patrilineal descent, were fatal weaknesses in successive Dynasties. Centralised dependence, coupled with the use of foreign generals to defend the borders allowing them to create distinct decentralised power bases, and the influence of Imperial consorts on the Emperor, led to the demise of the Han. The rise of consorts' families and the influence of the Court eunuchs created powerful inner threats to the throne. It guaranteed court intrigue and strife based on fear, greed and ambition. It was an inherent weakness of the system that the later T'ang also experienced.

Han China that existed for over four hundred years dissolved in rebellion, and was followed by a complex period of warring kingdoms and dynasties that lasted from 220 to 589AD. Taoism as a philosophy of retreat and self-cultivation flourished in this Age of Division. As did Buddhism born in India but introduced to China by 65AD. It offered a philosophy of enlightenment, based on an analysis of suffering and the renunciation of attachment to the world. It had affinities of attitude with Taoism in its quietism, disengagement, and disciplined spirituality. It involved compassion, release from caste and gender distinctions, and the superiority of the private mind to the public persona.

Taoism and Buddhism with an accretion of icons, divinities, magical practices, temples, and scriptures, became popular religions. Through the latter part of this period of instability, the north and south were politically separate. Northern China laid strong emphasis on Confucian ideals and ethics, on mastery of the histories and classics, and on public service. The Southern aristocracies encouraged a literary and artistic world where the life of convivial conversation, and the practise of calligraphy, poetry and painting, led to intellectual artistic sensibility being valued highly. Throughout the period China retained a common language and culture that was enriched and developed in a more personal way, and this continuity offset the effects of continual disorder and dislocation, and preserved the desire for strong, centralised government as a means to ensure peace and stability.

T'ao Chien (also called Tao Yüan-ming, 365-427AD) is the great southern poet of this period. He is the fully formed individual, quitting political life to live in the quietist Taoist manner on his small tract of land. His poetry is the poetry of friendship and family, enjoyment of music, wine, and literature, withdrawal from public affairs, and immersion in the rational cultivation of art, nature and the self. He provided an archetype for later men of letters. He is the self-contained single one who finds a way to live undisturbed by external events and in harmony with nature.

Singing Alone in a Wintry Mountain, Liang Yuwei（d. 1912）

THE NATURE OF THE TAO

The Tao is the impersonal anonymous neutral matrix underpinning every manifestation. It is the nature of reality and the means by which the universe operates. In terms of Western science we could call it Energy. The *manifestations* of it would be the entities of the microcosmic world of particle physics, the objects and processes of the macrocosm, and the configurations of forces and forms in which those energies can appear through time. What is its *reality*? Well what *is* energy or force? What *is* gravity or inertia? What *is* a sub-atomic particle? We can only reply with *how* things work and move and configure and change. We can only answer with observation and theory. The *'what'* is forever mysterious, untouchable, numinous. It is the given. We employ names to try and describe it, like substance, matter, and force. We can manipulate their symbols within a mathematical framework and thereby describe the transformations of energy, but the world itself is forever as it appears to us, and no more. Reality *is* appearance.

Who is satisfied with that? We *know*, irrationally, that appearances are illusion and deception while realities are fundamental and independent of our existence. We *know* the world is real. But we cannot truly name or touch that which makes it so. Modern physics attempts through mathematics to model and thereby describe the intangible and ambiguous nature of the subatomic quantum world whose particle nature exists alongside its probabilistic wave nature with complementary validity.

We fail in any attempt to visualise what the 'real' entity is that can be described by alternative and radically different mathematics, described that is as probability wave *and* particle. It is in one sense a bounded form observed to be at a fairly precise location in space with a fairly precise velocity. In another sense it only exists as a continuum of energy, giving a statistical likelihood of an entity being observed as a tightly bounded form, at any particular fairly precise location with a fairly precise velocity. Measurement of both velocity and position simultaneously is thwarted in the act of observation and this uncertainty principle emphasises the strangeness of the quantum universe. We cannot even say that the unobserved particle is in any place at all. Observation gives it reality for us.

As we examine dynamic systems like water or clouds we discover bounded but non-repeating patterns, and random fluctuation. When we examine natural shapes there are infinite levels, endless scaling, of precise fractal detail, and there are sudden transitions. Weather patterns may progress in a stately fashion then non-linear changes allow tiny disturbances to initiate vast effects. Our lives rely on bounded and unambiguous entities and processes, yet at the core of the quantum universe, and of unstable systems, is chance, an intrinsic randomness that is of the very nature of reality. At the microcosmic level we rely on the statistical probabilities of ambiguous event expressed in mathematical terms. In fluid systems like water or clouds we do find self-referencing structure. But we still exist in a universe of turbulent flow, of whorls and spirals, entanglement and elusiveness. There is infinite detail in finite spaces. There are infinite lines in bounded areas. The river remains, but the currents shift, and the water patterns vary endlessly. The cloudbank passes over, but its clouds separate and recombine, and their configurations alter continuously.

If we can free ourselves from the idea that there are only fixed forms, clear boundaries, nameable entities, and ultimate certainties then we enter the world of the Tao. The Tao encompasses the fixed and the nameable as manifestations of energy, but the totality is fluid, unnameable and ultimately random. This is what it means to say that the Tao is indifferent: that it is directionless: that it is formless: that it is uncarved: that it is a matrix: that it is the spirit of the feminine: that it gives rise to the myriad creatures. The Tao is not reducible to its components and its manifestations: it encompasses them. 'Silent and empty, alone and unchanging, it has no name' says Lao Tzu 'so I call it the Way.' 'The Way is empty but nothing can fill it.' 'Without possession, without demands, without authority it is mysterious virtue.'

The Tao is behind that ceaseless flow of process and pattern that we see in nature, where nature is the universe untouched by the human. Within the water and the clouds are vortices of energy. Within the bounded object are random flickering patterns of underlying sub-atomic structure. The boundaries are continually eroding and altering. We also are a part of nature, where nature is the totality that includes us. Every human being is a continuously changing network of energies and forms. The mind is a set of parallel hierarchical processes. The instant, the object, the thought, the movement, the world itself are impermanent. Every moment is a unique configuration of what is. The past configuration neither exists nor returns. The future configuration does not yet exist and is in its entirety unknowable. The moment is itself imprecise. The configuration is itself ungraspable. Name it and it shifts. Grasp it and it changes. Like clouds in the wind, like water in the river, the reality is evanescent, a vast movement, a loosely connected web. Things that last long enough to be named make up our useful world of reliable objects, discernible process, and stable patterns. They are the myriad creatures. The Tao is uncarved: a feminine matrix. 'The spirit of the valley never dies' says the Tao Te Ching 'its name is the mysterious feminine. The mysterious feminine is called the root of heaven and earth.'

山如臥屏樹
游龍遙影清
溪入畫容夢
到華香間草
橛隔几公用白
雪封
青汁道人

Reflections in a Clear Stream, Cheng Zhengkui (1604 – 1676)

TAOISM AND T'AO CH'IEN

What did Taoism mean in ancient China as a way of life? Taoism is a mental attitude. It is not a system of thought because it denies the validity of systemisation. It is not a religion because in its pure form it has no use for divinities. It is not a rigorous discipline because it seeks to evade inappropriate goal-driven behaviour. Analysis and definition, naming and theorising are anathema to it. Taoism denies the validity of the scientific project. It denies the validity of the work ethic. It denies the usefulness of ambitions and desires, grasping and craving. To those who say 'My life feels empty' Taoism would respond by saying 'That is because you are trying to fill it.' To those who say 'My life is without purpose' Taoism would reply 'That is because you are trying to give it a purpose.' The only aim of Taoism is to be in harmony with the Tao, with inner and outer nature. The result of that harmony is tranquillity. It can only be achieved, if at all, through relinquishing hold, through comprehending the flow of the universe, through discarding the superfluous, through eliminating inappropriate desires. It involves respect for *wu-wei* that is inaction and non-intervention. It can be approached through *tzu-jan,* spontaneity. Its movements are like a flag in the wind, or a ball on a mountain stream. Taoism despite this is in no way world-rejecting. The Taoist is independent, self-sufficient. The Taoist works as necessary to sustain his or her life, and stops when he or she has achieved the essential. The Taoist takes pleasure in things that are harmless, which connect to the flow of nature and the Tao. The Taoist acts only when it is valuable to do so, and desists when the effect has been achieved.

In the arts the Way is simplicity within subtlety. In everyday life the Way is balance within moderation. It encourages retreat and withdrawal, silence and stillness but is neither hostile nor humourless. The Taoist is moral because the Taoist life is both non-intrusive and non-grasping. Equally the Taoist does not proselytise or seek to convince, offers compassion but does not set out on a mission to relieve suffering. Non-involvement leaves others free. The Way is open to anyone who finds it. The Taoist tends the field and garden, tries to follow nature, and attempts to achieve and create harmony.

There are some similarities with the aspirations and practices of the Vedantic Yoga schools. There is a like emphasis on discriminating between the transient creatures and the permanent Tao: on renouncing futile activity and adopting a stance of *wu wei*, non-action, the passivity of the Yin. But where Yogic thought yearns for disengagement the Taoist merely disengages. Where Yogic practise strives for control of the self, through restraint, discontinuance of desired but inappropriate activity, indifference to the polar opposites, concentration, and faith, the Taoist forgets the self altogether and is absorbed into the natural. Taoism is a simple acceptance and acquiescence, a lyrical and harmonious attitude of mind that rejects the absurdities of the creature striving always to create something alien, the human opposed to nature. It avoids and eludes whatever damages or destroys tranquillity of mind and spiritual peace. It sees the human best exemplified in the sincerity and simplicity of the tiny infant. The true spirit keeps a child's heart.

'There are four things that do not leave people in peace' says the Lieh Tzu 'trying to live for ever, needing to be known, wanting high status, desiring wealth.....their lives are controlled by the external. But those who accept their destiny do not desire to endlessly prolong life, those who love honour do not need fame, those who reject power do not want status, and those who are without strong desires have no use for wealth... these people live according to internal things.'

There is a story of the Zen Master who passed on to his only disciple the famous and valuable text that had been annotated and handed down for seven generations from master to master. 'You had better keep it if it is so valuable, said the disciple 'I am satisfied as I am.' 'I know that, but even so' said the Master 'you must keep it. Here.' Feeling its sudden weight in his hands the disciple instantly flung it into the fire. 'What are you doing, what are you doing!' shouted the Master. 'What are you saying, what are you saying?' replied the disciple.

'Find your true face' said Hui-neng the sixth patriarch of Zen 'the one you had before you were born'. It is the self that is un-carved, in front of that universe that is unnameable. Then there is no need for religions or moral codes. Released, the crystal child of the self defeats the great dragon. As in Buddhist thought, the Wheel turns in the sky without being turned.

Everything becomes in itself spontaneous reality. It is as it is, without mind or nature. Taoism is the way to live a life on earth, respecting the body and the mind, existing simply, naturally, and harmoniously, in peace, as a free spirit. And there is consequently lightness, calm, and tolerance, a balance and a depth, reflected in Taoist art and literature.

T'ao Ch'ien [p. 119] (365-427AD) was one of the poets whose life exemplified the practise of the Taoist Way. He was a minor official but later withdrew from public involvement. He celebrated the relinquishment of that life where he viewed himself as having been 'too long a prisoner, captive in a cage'. He writes about a quiet way of existence, among friends and family, about the practise of simple pleasures, creating poems, cultivating his land, and enjoying natural beauty. His poetry is like a Sung Dynasty landscape painting with himself a tiny figure in the scene. Drinking wine is a means of escaping excessive introspection. Enjoying nature without intervening in it is a means of escaping analysis and definition. The private rather than the public life satisfies and the personal is enough, while the Tao is intrinsically unknowable and wordless.

The Taoist life is centred on nature. No separation is conceived between the sacred and profane, there are only the harmonious and the inharmonious. A human being is one of the myriad creatures, modest in scale. Conformity with the Tao, with the order of the universe, is all that is necessary to the true life. Therefore the Taoist does not seek to change the natural except in accord with absolute necessity. Nature is not to be despoiled for inappropriate material gain. The Taoist needs neither ambitions nor moral code. The Taoist may be a recluse living in the hills, a wanderer among mountains and rivers, a gardener or a poet, in a humble occupation, or free of all except essential occupation. The Taoist cultivates detachment from the world's affairs and concern for the unchanging and eternal. The Taoist embraces the mysterious and feminine, the dark and evanescent, the indistinct and rarified, the empty and minute, the tentative and hesitant, the turbid and vacant, the childishly simple and the foolishly obvious, the muddled and indifferent, the shapeless and dim.

T'ao Ch'ien reveals that absence of analysis, in his poems, that is the essence of Tao. It is not an absence of profundity. The deep is simple. The profound is obvious. He is without complex logic and artificial rhetoric. He is without conformity but without pride. He rejects power in order to be weak, and discipline in order to be natural, but he is neither undisciplined nor subservient, neither immoral nor crude. His foolishness is full of intelligence. His simplicity is not uncultivated. His weakness cannot be manipulated. His naturalness is imbued with ethical understanding.

In the first of his two poems titled 'Returning to Live in the Country' [p. 121] he evokes that life which evades public confusion to live in accord with nature and the true self. Elements of nature, mountains and hills, trees and streams, are mentioned but not described. They are there to point towards the Tao not to analyse it. The names of natural features are designed to evoke the natural framework not to provide complex metaphors. The Vortex is subtly present, as air, water, smoke, mist, and winding lanes. The life described is simple. The human need is in the end the same as that of other creatures, birds or fish. It is the freedom the caged bird wants or the fish in its pool. It allows the mind to achieve 'space and silence'.

In *the second poem* [p. 122] it is human transience which is the theme and by implication the continuum of nature. That which has vanished is set against the continuity of that which endures. The myriad creatures are contrasted with the eternal Vortex of the natural world.

His poem 'Drinking the Wine' [p. 124] evokes the inner silence of the Taoist. It endorses the simplicity of life, the satisfaction to be had in appreciation of natural beauty, the tranquillity gained by release from action, the elusiveness and indefinability of the Tao. Wine is a way to release spontaneity, to forget the world, to become part of the Way. It is a formal irresponsibility! The poem points to the unknowable essence of the natural world and therefore of life itself, where knowing what things do never takes us to what they inescapably are, never enables us to get at their whatness, their 'quiddity'. That they are - is mysterious. Though we push and poke at matter, though we study and analyse process, their reality in the vortex always gleams beyond us. Existence is not an attribute of things. The poem expresses the indifferent placidity of the Vortex. Filled with energy, a raging torrent, it is nevertheless detached, neutral. It is the calm surface without hostility even while it is the ceaseless movement without benevolence. Language and intellectual analysis do not get us closer to the essence. It is beyond mind and words. The landscape of the poem is one of remoteness, minuteness, and rarefaction. The hills are distant, the flights of birds dwindle, the air is thinned. Light is about to fade. 'Blunt the sharp' says the Tao Te Ching 'untie the knots, dim the glare.'

'Reading the Classic of Hills and Seas'[p. 123] is again a poem of the simple life. 'One glance finds all of heaven and earth'. T'ao Ch'ien points back to a passage from the Tao Te Ching on the virtues of non-action. The way of life recommended is neither spiritually lazy nor parasitic. The Taoist cultivates the land and garden, has an artistic sensibility and appreciation, develops the self but has compassion for others. If tranquillity is denied because one is caught in the world's net, it can still be an aspiration and a focus of personal values. 'Without going out, one can know the world. Without looking out, one can see the way. The further we go the less we know. Therefore the wise see without stirring, know without looking, achieve without doing'.

The Taoists frequently tease the Confucians. They see them as compelled to wander about in order to find employment and office, 'perching here and perching there'. Trapped in meaningless ritual and formal law. Forced to bow to those who are their inferiors in mind and morality. 'Even for a sack of rice a month it is not worth bending to this man' said T'ao Chien. 'Foolish to follow convention and propriety slavishly.' Confucian benevolence was, to the Taoist, a recipe for intrusive intervention in a world that was beyond human direction. 'As for you' said a Taoist to Confucius's follower Tzû Lu, 'instead of chasing after a leader who runs from one place to another you should rather follow those who escape the world entirely.'

Confucianism's articulation of rites and duties is a constriction of the natural self. The intelligent should pursue their own harmony, do not require to be instructed, embrace an intuitive ethics of moderation, and avoid evils by eliminating unnecessary desires. Ssû-ma Ch'ien the great Han historian tells a story of Confucius visiting Lao Tzu at Loyang and praising the ancient sages. 'Those you talk about are all dead' replied Lao Tzu 'and their bodies are turned to dust, only words are left. Get rid of your pride and your desires, your insinuating ways and your ambition. They are of no use to you. This is all I have to say.'

The Taoist stories are of those who reject office rather than disturb their equilibrium. 'Better to be a live tortoise dragging your tail in the mud', said Chuang-tzu on being pressed to return to Imperial service, 'than a dead tortoise sacred, and covered with jewels, in a box in the Emperor's palace.' Or of fishermen and recluses who laugh at the useless seriousness of the committed Confucian. The legendary fisherman knows that he has to paddle in the world's waters but should still wash eyes and ears in the clear stream of the Tao. He laughs and vanishes.

The sense of another world untouched by corruption is at the heart of T'ao Ch'ien's story of the *Peach Blossom Spring* [p. 126], that stream which leads the fisherman to a world of happy immortals living in harmony and having no desire to return to a world they have eluded. It is a story that is akin to the Western tales of worlds of faery, where the marvellous is commonplace and where tragedy is to lose the vision. Here the remote land is lost but remains an aspiration.

There is another story of Confucius and his pupils walking by a river that pours with immense power over the falls, and winds through the rocks. They see an old man, upstream, dive into the foam and vanish and they rush to save him. But there he is standing by the bank, unharmed, streaming with water. Confucius asks him how he could survive the force of the torrent. He replies, smiling, 'That's easy. I go down with the descending currents, and I come up with the ascending ones.' The Taoist aspiration is to achieve that spontaneity and careless calm, to accept, and not to struggle needlessly, to do the minimum in order to achieve the maximum.

The poet Hsi K'ang (223-262AD), writing a letter, explains his indifference to office and the attitude of the Taoist individual. 'He acts in harmony with his own nature and stops wherever he is at peace. Some people enter the Court and never set foot out of it. Others go into the mountains and never look back.... Wandering among rivers and hills, watching the birds in the leaves and looking at the fish in the water, is my greatest pleasure.... Ignoring status and fame, eliminating desire, making my mind still, my greatest goal is non-action... To keep to the simple ways, help my children and grandchildren, sit and talk with friends, drink wine, play music, this is the height of my needs and ambitions.'

Fishermen on Snowy River, Lu Mingqian (1744)

THE T'ANG DYNASTY

At the end of the sixth century north and south were reunited by northern military power and the Sui Dynasty was founded. Within forty years it was destroyed by rebellion and replaced by the T'ang (618-907AD). The T'ang Dynasty was one of the great ages of development and consolidation in China. It looked back to other periods of transformation and cultural flowering, the ancient Dynasties of Shang and Chou, and the historical achievements of Ch'in and Han.

The Empire re-established strong central government based on the Imperial Court and on officials, trained in the Confucian Classics for public service. These officials formed an intellectual elite loyal to the throne. The borders expanded and China's cultural influence extended to Japan in the east and to Korea, and Vietnam in the southeast. Sogdiana and Transoxiana, across the mountains of the Tian Shan and the Pamirs in Central Asia, became areas of military contention. Trade routes ran through them to the west and south. Southern sea-routes also stimulated foreign trade and cultural imports, as well as an influx of immigrant traders, artisans and students. Persians, Indians, Syrians, Africans, and Greeks all found their way to the capitals at Ch'ang-an and Lo-yang, introducing a vital cosmopolitan influence. There was substantial contact with Europe and Arabia as well as Persia and India.

It was an empire of around 50 million people and centralisation on the twin capitals gave Ch'ang-an a population of a million people, the largest city concentration in the world, and Lo-yang a population of three quarters of a million. This concentration further unified Chinese culture, and allowed it to rapidly absorb foreign artistic influences, music and dance from Asia, and new verse forms.

T'ai Tsung (reigned 626-649AD), the second T'ang Emperor, initiated a period of construction both at home and in foreign policy. Border strategy based on strong fortifications encouraged trade along the Silk Routes in Central Asia. The T'ang Code of 653AD standardised the laws. The centre controlled and rotated provincial officers limiting the power of the provincial elites. The civil-service examinations were extended to encourage Confucian values and create a loyal cadre dedicated to public responsibility and ethical values. This system encouraged a search for talent though it remained dominated by the famous aristocratic families. Low but comprehensive taxation encouraged economic growth and brought nine million families into the tax system. Unification of north and south was aided by the continuous engineering of the Grand Canal system, built with conscripted labour, linking the Eastern capital Lo-yang to the Yangtze valley and then pushing northeast as well as further south. The canal extended twelve hundred miles with a parallel Imperial road and bridges and with relay post stations enabling long-distance supply of the army.

By the middle of the seventh century China was a dynamic, cosmopolitan Empire, trading internationally, with an ordered agrarian population benefiting from land-share, two massive capitals, an educated, artistic and creative elite, and strong borders. Towards the later part of the century the Court was under the dominance of the Empress Wu, who began her career as a concubine of the Emperor. She is an example of those women in Chinese Imperial history who from the role of concubine exerted tremendous influence over the reigning monarch, and who gained power for themselves and through the promotion of their families. The monarchy was always vulnerable to the power group from within.

She controlled the monarchy and the succeeding reigns of her two sons, whom she deposed, proclaiming herself Emperor of a new dynasty in 690AD and claiming to be a reincarnation of the Buddha Maitreya as a female ruler. Tough and uncompromising she maintained a robust foreign policy and quelled internal dissent until she was finally deposed in 705 when over eighty and in ill health. The T'ang was immediately restored and in 712 her grandson Hsüang Tsung, Ming Huang the Glorious Monarch, came to the throne.

For fifty years, in a history that spans four thousand years, Chinese civilisation achieved a peak of cultural sophistication. T'ang China is the land of peonies and plum-blossom, moonlight and green jade, where dragons live in the lakes and turn into pine trees, where gauze-sleeved dancing girls glance from beneath green painted willow eyebrows, where peach-trees and mulberries talk to cedar and bamboo. It is the land of silk and cinnabar, cassia and pearl, a country, perfect in the mind, which the West could not have invented if it had not already existed. Tea, fine rain, lake views, gardens with curious rocks, girls with gauze veils and gowns, boxes of tortoise-shell and gold, and also, behind the Imperial splendour, a vast country of villages and farms, mountains and rivers littered with the remnants of earlier dynasties. A land where Buddhism, Taoism and Confucianism blended in the civilised mind in complementary subtlety. A land of technology without science, of the seismograph and the armillary sphere, magnetism and the compass, the continuous bellows and steel-making, paper and printed books, the movable stern-post rudder and vast sailing ships. A land of *literati* and connoisseurs, of painters and poets, of courtesans and concubines, of lute and zither, pipe and drum.

The core T'ang territories were in Central China. They lay between the Wei and Yellow (Hwang Ho) Rivers in the north and the Yangtse River in the south. These are the two great water systems that cross China from the high mountains of the west to the eastern seas. On the western side of this central box, the Kialing River runs southwards from hills below the Wei to meet the Yangtze at Chungking. In the centre the tributaries and lower reaches of the Han River also run southeast reaching the Yangtze near Hankow. The Han River therefore marks out the highlands of the west from the flood plains of the east. On the eastern side of the box are the provinces of Shantung and Kiangsu and the Yellow Sea.

While the centres of administrative power lay to the north and west in the two capitals of Ch'ang-an and Loyang, and the great rivers had many obstacles to navigation, it was still possible to travel extensively across eastern and southern China. Imperial roads and canals could be used wherever they existed, as well as the open stretches of the rivers. Li Po in his wanderings visited many of the towns of the north-eastern, eastern and southern provinces, Peking and Kai-feng in the north, Yangchow, Nanking, Kuikiang and Hankow in the south. Routes led to the West also. From Ch'ang-an in Shensi, the western capital on the Wei River, ran the route to Central Asia to the northwest. Across the mountains and rivers to the southwest lay Szechwan and the headwaters of the Yangtze, often a place of exile. The capital of Szechwan, Chêng-tu, Brocade City, though it was difficult of access from Ch'ang-an, lies in the Red Basin, immensely fertile land surrounded by hills and mountains. The 'bread-basket' of China, the

Red Basin, was an ancient inland-sea. The Yangtze tributaries were canalised and cleared by Ch'in engineers and labour in 250BC. Canals, dykes and dams regulated the mountain waters to build the silt layers that fertilise the Basin. Chêng-tu was later the capital of the Kingdom of Shu (221-263AD). Li Po, who as a child was brought up northeast of Chêng-tu, wrote a poem about climbing the high passes to reach it from the northeast. 'Shu Way is hard! Shu Way is high! Like climbing to Heaven, climbing the Szechwan Road.'

Ch'ang-an the western capital had been the capital of the Han from 202BC, sited a few miles from the previous Ch'in capital burnt to the ground during the rebellion that brought the Han to power. To look back from Sui and T'ang to Ch'in and Han was to look back to a time of greatness, to the time of the building of the Great Wall and the expansion of the borders. In Han times Ch'ang-an provided a concentration of rich and influential families, with a common Chinese language and culture, living within a stable centralised system, and the T'ang Renaissance recreated this.

Ch'ang-an, (modern Xian or Sian), was sited on the banks of the sluggish Wei River, fifty miles from the junction of the Wei and the Yellow River, north of the Ch'in-ling Mountains and with the T'ai-hang mountains to the east. Its periods of stability and continuity were punctuated by the tremors of war and rebellion. Sacked in 26AD by the Red-Eyebrow guerrillas it was re-established in 191AD to be sacked again in 311 and was rebuilt by the Sui Dynasty in 583.

In T'ang times the rectangular walled city, its sides oriented to the points of the compass, was laid out like a giant chessboard, a grid of a hundred and eight walled wards closed at night, with markets, Buddhist and Taoist monasteries, and Manichean, Mazdean and Nestorian temples. The outer walls, entered and exited through great gates with flanking towers, were made of pounded earth sixteen metres thick at the base and eight metres high. The rectangle of the city extended over eight kilometres north to south and over nine kilometres east to west, to cover over eighty square kilometres containing a population of a million people. The Imperial City with lakes and pools extended south from the northern wall. Its position placed the apartments of the consorts and concubines in the Yin north. It faced the Yang south and the administrative city that in turn looked out to the city wards. To the northeast of the city was the Ta Ming palace and the

Imperial Park. To the northwest of the city was the Emperor's summer palace. In the southeast corner of the city were the Hibiscus Garden and the 'Serpentine' Lake. Outside the Western Wall was the Shang-lin complex designed in Han times with gardens, halls and palaces. In one of the ornamental lakes Emperor Wu of Han had built a model of the mythical P'eng-lai Palace on the Islands of the Blessed in the Eastern Seas. The southern gate opened out on to a broad avenue that, like others of the city's great avenues, was edged by ditches planted with trees. The Great and Little Swallow Pagodas towered into the sky. In the K'un-ming Pool near the city, constructed for Naval exercises was a famous statue of a whale, and near it statues of the Weaver Girl and the Herdboy, whose annual meeting in the starry sky guaranteed the cyclic movement of the cosmos.

The Wei River valley past Ch'ang-an was the main trade corridor from China to Central Asia, a continuation of the Yellow River route from Honan province. Trade goods flowed to and from India and the West along the line of towns and oases forming the Silk Road. Caravans heading west from Ch'ang-an travelled the Kansu 'long corridor', the great 'valley' where the Han race originated, skirting the Gobi Desert to the north and the Nan Shan mountains to the southwest. The Jade Gate, at the old town of Yumen, piercing the Great Wall, allowed them exit to Tun-huang on the edge of the Tarim Basin.

Back through the gate passed high quality raw jade, from the mountains further west, down into China. From Tun-huang they entered the hostile and arid Basin where a number of alternative routes ran west along the northern and southern edges of the Basin's barren Taklamakan Desert. There they skirted the eight-hundred-mile sea of sand dunes, lying between the Tien Shan (Celestial Mountains) range to the north and the Kunlun range to the south. One route passed by Lop Nor's lake to reach Loulan, where the caravans could provision before heading west along the Tarim River system. Reaching Kashgar at the other end of the Tarim Basin, travellers could then cross the northern edge of the Pamirs via the Terek and other passes to Fergana. Then along the chain of oases, Samarkand, Bokhara, Merv, and on to Baghdad, the Middle East and Europe. This was the trade corridor between Rome and the Han Empire.

Itinerant Buddhist monks joined the caravans along the Silk Road bringing their literature and way of life, creating the Buddhist cave complexes at Tun-huang and K'u-ch'e. They could reach Khotan in the Tarim Basin from the Indus valley to the south by crossing the Hindu Kush, over the frozen eighteen thousand-foot heights of the Karakoram Pass. This route along the south of the Tarim Basin between Khotan and Loulan was the path taken by Hsüan-tsang the Chinese Buddhist pilgrim in 629AD, who spent sixteen years travelling from China through India and returned bringing copies of key Buddhist texts. His experiences are the theme of one of China's few long novels, 'The Journey to the West' (Xijouyi). Travelling to the south of the Taklamakan, he no doubt experienced the *karaburan* or black hurricane, a dark storm of pebbles and sand lasting for hours. 'At times you hear melancholy wails and pitiful cries, and, between the sight and sounds of the desert, men are confused and lost. So many people die on the way, the work of evil spirits and demons.'

Manicheanism, Nestorian Christianity, Judaism, Mohammedanism, and Zoroastrianism entered China along the Silk Road. Envoys from Sassanid Persia, Byzantium, and Arabia had reached Ch'ang-an by the seventh century. And as well as the traffic to the west, there was extensive sea-trade with Japan, and coastal traffic with Korea and South-East Asia. China absorbed immigrants and refugees, Arabs and North Africans, pilgrims from India, Turkoman nomads, Jewish and Muslim merchants. Ch'ang-an's cosmopolitan population imported foreign jewels and silver, horses and textiles, raw materials and ceramics. It copied foreign fashions in clothing and hairstyles, furniture and art-objects, song and dance. New instruments and musical forms changed the Chinese native models. The Uighurs, the Turkomans of Urumqui and Turfan, produced famous wine, sending the ice-packed golden grapes called 'mares teats' and the best musicians and dancers of Asia to Ch'ang-an. Wealth and leisure demanded performing artists in dance, mime, music and song, and Asian songs and ballad forms stimulated new poetic patterns in the works of the intellectual elite.

The rich officials and aristocrats of the city also had second homes in the country. To the south east of the capital was the Lant'ien (Indigo Fields) prefecture where the wealthy had their extensive retreats in the Chungnan (South Mountain) foothills and along the Wang River. Wang Wei the poet painter had a famous estate here. It was a pleasant place for weary officials to escape to, where they could satisfy the desire to be close to Nature's force and beauty amongst relaxing scenery.

Lo-yang the eastern capital, two hundred miles from Ch'ang-an, also had its lakes and palaces, gardens and temples. With a population of three-quarters of a million it stood at the gateway to the great flood plains of the Yellow River. Less well-defended and smaller than Ch'ang-an, but with better water supplies, it was sited on the north bank of the Lo River and south of the Yellow River in Honan province. Built by the Chou it was the Eastern Han capital from 25AD and was sacked along with Ch'ang-an in 311AD though rebuilt in the 490's. It too was re-established by the Sui Dynasty. When Empress Wu came to the T'ang throne she had a Hall of Light, a Ming-t'ang built there, to symbolise the power of the dynasty. Three tiered, its lowest tier symbolised the four seasons, the second tier the twelve double hours with a dish-shaped roof supported by nine dragons, and the highest tier symbolised the twenty-four fortnights of the year.

Landscape, Jin Kan (d. 1703)

T'ANG CHINA

The Chinese poets give glimpses of the life of Ch'ang-an's Imperial Palace. The beauty of Hibiscus Park, with its memories of the Han consorts. The crystal blinds, embroidered curtains, silk and mica screens of the Imperial apartments and terraces. The lakes and pools with their stone ornaments, fish and dragons. Lutes and pipes sounding through the gardens. The flowered skirts, the jade pendants, the gauze and crimson silks, the slender waists and green-painted willow eyebrows, of girls dancing. Wine drinking in the moonlight. Candles and silk fans, kingfisher covers and carved mirrors. Midnight visits and the exchange of poems. Scented robes and letters on coloured paper. Water clocks and chiming bells. Lacquered trays and cups. Gardens of bamboos and cassia, willows and chrysanthemums, orchids and pear trees. Mandarin ducks and lotus flowers are on the waters, orioles are in the trees, butterflies over the grasses. The cry of the phoenix sounds, and eyes are filled with tears. There is a coolness of jade and pearl. There is a rustle of silk over dew-white steps.

Chang Hêng describes the dancers of Huai-nan. 'Delicate snapping waists, a glow of the lotus flower, shedding crimson flame. Languid hesitant eyes, suddenly blaze with light, skirts fluttering, birds in flight. Gauze sleeves whirl falling snow, weaving the dancing hours, till white powder and willow brows are gone, flushed faces, tangled hair, gathered and held with combs. Gowns of gossamer trail. Perfect the harmony, sound, figures and dress.' 'Music that falls from the white clouds' says Li Po. 'The sound of the flutes drifting from shore to shore.'

T'ang China's immense influence on Japanese culture echoes in the Tale of Genji, Murasaki Shikibu's poetic novel set sometime in the Heian period of the ninth and tenth centuries AD. Picking up the theme of the Emperor captivated by a concubine from the T'ang, the Tale of Genji enters a similar world of midnight assignations, neglected women, aesthetic appreciation, and reticent, subtle feeling. 'What men wanted was women not of high station but with true and delicate sensibilities who would hint to them of their feelings through poems and letters as the clouds passed and the blossom and grasses flowered and faded.' To the Buddhists, Confucians and true Taoists this was a marred world of sensuality and attachment, of foolish intoxication and dangerous refinement. It is a world which the T'ang poets move in, and whose passing, with all its faults, they regret. The aesthetic easily slips into the sensual. Beauty appreciated in flowers, rivers, trees and mountains, in moonlight and stars, is also appreciated in women and wine, music and dance. Courtesans and dancing girls are the subject of many delicate poems that often stress loneliness and neglect, misplaced affection and fading beauty. Li Po 'would take his singing girls Chin-ling and Chao-yang with him on his journeys'. And 'when he was drunk his page boy Cinnabar would play the Waves of the Blue Ocean', the tune that Genji danced to in front of the Emperor so that he 'seemed not of this world'. It is a beautiful, wasteful, clinging, suspect atmosphere, seductive and delightful, but confusing the mind and absorbing the senses. It entices with the joy of youthful faces and deludes with the transience of passing things.

In T'ang China the intoxicating beauty and subsequent neglect of women is a charged theme. A social role based on sexual availability and feminine beauty and talents did not carry the stigma of the West but equally did involve the risks and uncertainties of a precarious life. Concubines of the Emperor or a wealthy lord might see him seldom if at all and be effectively imprisoned within the life of the harem. It was often seen as an immoral practice by sections of the educated classes, being unnatural and dangerous to good government while condemning the girls to a life of loneliness and neglect. Dancing girls might attract a man of wealth and become entangled only to see him vanish again. Taoism provided a refuge for daughters of high officials or these concubines put away by their lords. Many Taoist nuns were just such women, while others used their education, talents and connections to pursue a life as high-class courtesans.

Sexuality in itself carried no stigma but the predilection of the men for very young girls and the natural intensity of relationships still brought with it all the complexities, confusions and heartbreak of the transient or clandestine liaison. There is ambivalence about the stories of the obsessions of older men with young women. Were they in themselves pernicious relationships that in the case of the Emperor and high officials damaged the State, or could a private love matter more than the ruin of a kingdom?

There were many concubines and courtesans who were famous for their beauty and their relationships with the powerful, and their situation echoes through later Chinese and Japanese literature so that the names of the one evoke the other. There are therefore many analogues for Yang Kuei-fei. In the Han Dynasty there is the concubine of Emperor Ch'eng-ti, Lady Pan, put aside because of her humble birth and slanders spoken against her, in favour of the consort Fei Yen, or Flying Swallow, who was said to be so light and delicate she could dance on a man's palm. Lady Pan's fate was the subject of many poems including her own. Wang Wei's 'Three Songs for Lady Pan' [p. 154] is a set of variations on the theme. There is Hsi Shih, the most beautiful of women, legendary consort of King Wu, referred to by Li Po in 'The Roosting Crows [p. 184]'. There is Lu-chu, Green Pearl, Shih Chung's concubine in the third century AD who sang and danced for him at his famous estate at Golden Vale. There is Wang Chao-chün, concubine of Emperor Yüan of Han who gave her as wife to a Tartar Khan, and on whose tomb the grass was always green, or that earlier Chinese princess sent to a Tartar chieftain who yearned 'to be the yellow swan that returns to its home'. And in the Japanese Tale of Genji who follows 'the way of love' there is Genji's cluster of consorts, the Akashi Lady, the Lady of the Evening Face, the Safflower Lady, and the child Murasaki, 'the lavender that shares its roots with another's'. Li Po's poems *Jade Stairs Grievance* [p. 182] and *'Yearning'* [p. 183] capture the sadness, regret and longing of a frequently disappointed love. Emperor Wu-ti of the Liang Dynasty, he who invited the Buddhist Bodhidarma founder of the Ch'an (Zen) school to China, writes a love poem as if from the woman, as was the poetic convention. 'My dress fragrant still with the perfume you wore. My hand still touching the letter you sent.'

'Silk robes rustled as her women moved softly about.' 'The wind was rising.' says the Tale of Genji, 'The perfumed mystery of dark incense drifted over the blinds to mix with the faint altar incense and the fragrance of his own robes bringing intimations of the Western Paradise.' 'With the blinds still lifted the delicate scent of the plum blossoms blew in.'

Courtesans and concubines were often skilled in music. The T'ang poets generally used the verse form known as *shih*, basically five or seven syllable lines in paired couplets with the even lines rhyming. The five-syllable line is made up of two plus three syllables with a caesura or pause (a sigh) between them. The seven-syllable line is made up of four and three. These forms appeared in Ch'ang-an round about the first century AD introduced from the song and dance rhythms of professional girls, possibly from Persia and Central Asia. Li Po's *'Yearning'* [p. 183] displays a courtesan who is also a skilled musician.

The old-style *shih* poems developed into the highly regulated new style verse, the eight-line form with internal balancing and alternation of characters and tones. There were also four line 'stop-short' poems, the *yüeh-fu* ballad forms, and traditional songs. Poets were among those who frequented the entertainment quarters of the city like Heng-t'ang, entering the 'floating world' of the 'blue houses'. The singing and dancing girls, the female musicians and courtesans, composed songs and lyrics and sang and played the compositions of the educated men who visited them. Music and poetry were intermingled. In the case of Wang Wei his musicianship may have been on a par with both his poetry and his painting.

Landscape in the Style of Fan Kuan (14th – 15th century)

WANG WEI

Wang Wei [p. 127] was born in 699AD in Shensi province. His father was a local official, his mother a member of a distinguished literary family. He and his brother were introduced to society in the Capital when he was about sixteen years old. An early poem *'Words for the Mica Screen'* [p. 138] already shows the acute sensibility and light, quiet touch of the poet and painter. The transparent screen reveals the landscape as though it was a painting made by Nature. Behind the artifice is the reality that obviates the need for artifice. Nature is a better painter than humanity. Through art Nature can be shown and enhanced, but Nature is always beyond art as the greater existence that can only be reached by simplicity, sensitivity and attentiveness. This tension remains throughout Wang's work, the desire for expression and realisation counterbalanced by the knowledge that Nature should be sufficient. That feeling for the profundity of reality, that renders art superfluous and unnecessary, was a factor in Wang's attraction to Buddhism and led to a perpetual dissatisfaction with his artistic achievement that perhaps made him a greater poet and painter.

His lines *'Written on the Wang River Scroll'* [p. 160] acknowledge the 'error' of any perception of him as purely an artistic surface, and point to the elusiveness of the true self that is beyond art. He was drawn to the pleasures of art and creation, but also understood the Taoist ideal of non-action and a more profound passivity. Equally he is full of feelings, not expressed or inexpressible, below the surface of the poems, while trying to follow the Buddhist path to extinction of desire and self.

This early period also produced the poem on *'Peach Blossom Spring'* [p. 132], a retelling of T'ao Ch'ien's famous story. Here is the Taoist theme, of a truer life that can be achieved outside or beyond the contemporary world, a life that is found and too easily lost again, that is deep in the Yin reality symbolised by peach blossom and clouded woods, by the green stream and bright moon. There, human beings are free of intrusiveness, forget time, achieve simplicity, and become 'Immortals'. There, they cultivate their gardens outside the mainstream of events. As against the Confucian ideals of rational and benevolent engagement with the world this is escapism, and the land of Peach Blossom Spring is a 'refuge' from the unacceptable and inhuman world. But from a Taoist or Buddhist perspective it is a transcendence of the inhuman, a deeper existence. Since the goal human beings chase after is merely a transient illusion, then what is it an escape from, what is it an escape to?

In Wang's life and that of the other great poets, there is the tension between engagement and disengagement, between living in the suffering and feeling world, and living in the Vortex or the Void, between being a part and entering the mountains without looking back. From the perspective of the world, the Way is an escape, a turning away from what drives human affairs. From the perspective of the spirit however it is a realisation, an awakening, as in Ch'an (Zen) Buddhism, or a more gradual realisation of and eventual existence in harmony with the Tao, or a progression towards that extinction of the Self that is the Buddhist Nirvana.

When he was twenty-three in 722AD Wang Wei passed the *chin-shih*, the 'presented scholar' examination, which was a passport to official service. Introduced by the Sui Dynasty and elaborated by the T'ang the Civil Service examinations demanded a comprehensive knowledge of the Confucian Classics and also tested literary ability, including poetic composition. The Han Dynasty had encouraged officials who possessed moral integrity, intellectual ability, and respect for good manners, combined with the courage to speak out where the good of the State was at stake. It enabled the creation of a talented administrative elite controlled by the Imperial Court and therefore owing it allegiance, and in principle independent of other power-groups and factions. The Sui and T'ang strengthened and formalised this approach through the *chin-shih*, the 'degree of advanced learning' that aimed to find and promote men of intellect, integrity and culture.

Officials were therefore practising literary men, who had sufficient leisure to maintain sponsorship and practise of the arts, and whose concentration was on the cultured life (*wen*). In the mid eighth century the T'ang State Academy Directorate at Ch'ang-an had an enrolment of over two thousand students with a smaller version of the Directorate at Lo-yang. Though it recruited mainly from those with aristocratic backgrounds other candidates recognised as having great potential were also sponsored. The graduates of the system occupied about a seventh of the higher official executive posts including many of the key ones and formed a Court *élite*. Only twenty or thirty *chin-shih* students graduated successfully each year from about a thousand candidates, since the examinations demanded not only skill in two forms of composition and extensive ability to quote from the Confucian Classics, but also expert analysis of contemporary administrative and economic problems. Li Po never entered for the examination and Tu Fu did so but failed.

Wang was a man of multifarious talents, and he was immediately appointed to the Court, becoming the Assistant Secretary for Music. However he soon fell foul of the strict adherence to rules which officialdom required, and, through some minor error, was packed off to a lowly post in the provinces. 'Minor officials easily court trouble' he says in a poem, 'so here am I sent out to Chichou'. He stayed in Shantung for a few years before resigning and returning to Ch'ang-an. He married, and bought his beloved estate in the Chungnan foothills, south of the capital at Lant'ien, where he spent time whenever he could throughout his life. *'Leaving Wang River'* [p. 148] reveals his attachment to the solitude and spirituality that his retreat there allowed him, as though its reality was an echo of the Peach Blossom Paradise.

His wife died young when he was only thirty, and, though childless, he never remarried. One sad poem seems to refer to this difficult time. He entered public service again at the age of thirty-five. He then alternated his time between his official duties, including a mission to the north west frontier for three years in 737AD when he was thirty-eight (the poem *'Mission'* [p. 156] refers to this), and his life at his Wang River estate where he could paint and write, be musician and scholar. His poetry and painting is filled with the natural landscape and a deeply felt Taoist sympathy.

His poem *'A Reply'* [p. 135] for instance communicates the elusiveness of the mind that is lost in contemplation of natural beauty. *'Chungnan'* [p. 139] expresses his need for solitude and meditation relieved now and then by human companionship. Poems like these reveal the instinctive Taoist, the artist with great aesthetic sensibility whose response to Nature is empathetic. His aspiration is to be part of the natural world, to release the will, create spontaneously, think tranquilly, and merge with the perceived beauty. He became an archetype of the scholar-painter, and his genius allowed him to be appropriated later as the founder of the Southern School of landscape painting, though none of his paintings survive. The Wang River Scroll was particularly famous and showed twenty scenes around his estate with accompanying verses, the scroll form allowing the unrolling of an extended landscape and creating a new mode of depiction. Later landscape painting concentrates on natural harmony often to the exclusion of humankind, the human being represented by tiny figures in the landscape, lost amongst Yin valleys, clouds and rivers, Yang mountains, rocks and pines. Parts of the paint surface are often blank, using the emptiness of the underlying texture to generate a sense of the Tao. 'What we realise is Something' says the Tao Te Ching, 'but it is by using Nothing that we allow it to exist.' Hsieh Ho, at the end of the fifth century AD stated the six main techniques of painting. The first and most important being *ch'i-yün sheng-tung*, the achievement of an atmosphere and tone that is fully alive.

The painter should express a depth and clarity of spirit that is in sympathy with the natural world. The painting is created with spontaneity, harmony and vitality. It captures the essence of things. Kuo Hsi in the eleventh century said that painting depended on concentration, seriousness, lightness of spirit, and energy. This is the Taoist inner harmony and spontaneity, combined with a deep intuition of Nature, supported by technique, but ultimately capable of communicating despite blemishes of technique. Lack of harmony leaves art lifeless despite technical excellence.

'*Ch'i* means the mind guiding the brush in complete control', said the tenth century painter Ching Hao, 'When you picture the form but miss the spirit that is merely a likeness. The real essence is to capture the form *and* the spirit. When the spirit is missing the form is dead. To do it without apparent effort and catch the natural form is the work of a master.' 'Pictures are made in the mind' wrote Kuo Jo-hsü a great critic of the Sung Dynasty, 'they are expressed and revealed through the tip of the brush. The sense of the form of things is created mysteriously to rouse the feelings and awaken the greatness of mens' spirits.' Shen Tsung-ch'ien in the eighteenth century talks about the need for sureness of touch and firmness of line. '*Ch'i* (breath, spirit, atmosphere or here force) is all-important in applying the brush. Force gives strength to the stroke and any line drawn is alive with energy. We say the line has spirit.' The artist by embracing Taoist spontaneity allied to technical capability can meditate to escape the self-conscious desire to create, and in doing so can create in a deeper mode than that achievable by mere knowledge and effort. It is a mode of inspiration, since *ch'i* is precisely spirit, vital spirit, or breath. Combined with technical excellence it achieves greatness.

We no longer have any original paintings by Wang, but he is said to have painted with sensitive, thin lines with delicate, additional line-shading emphasising fine detail. Forms and colours blurred in the distance in fluid atmosphere. The use of rhythmic lines with emphasis on contour and texture, rather than the use of ink shading as in the West, is a feature of much of later Chinese painting. A ninth century writer Chang Yen-yüan mentions Wang for the depth of his paintings. Ching Hao talks about his harmonious brushstrokes, elevated tone, and deep knowledge of forms. Mi Fei, the great eleventh century painter, mentions seeing a self-portrait by Wang in a yellow robe, with palms together, that he states as genuine. He also comments that any paintings with delicate lines are too freely ascribed to Wang, for example snow scenes, and he protests at this indiscriminate mis-attribution of inferior paintings in order to enhance their value.

Wang is claimed as the author of two early treatises on painting technique and traditionally he is held to be the inventor of monochrome ink landscape painting. The Ch'an Buddhist School was to develop monochrome in a penetrating and profound way to express the meditative atmosphere from which Buddhist enlightenment was achieved. Using multi-toned Chinese black ink on paper or silk it combined calligraphy, imitating 'grass writing', with the vital immediacy of the spontaneous brush stroke. The hand flows over the surface in a continuous movement combining grace, strength, rapidity, fluidity and lightness of touch.

Wang seems to have used a more restrained, but harmonious technique, that led to him being viewed as the founder of the later 'Southern School'. He no doubt helped that concentration on pure landscape, the 'mountains and waters' motif that became the favourite theme of Chinese art alongside 'flowers and birds', 'bamboo in ink' and 'quadrupeds and plants'. All the elements of a painting were designed to evoke the flow of natural energies, the dragon veins of rocks, the flickering life of birds, the graceful interlacing of flowers and leaves in the breeze, the movement of water, the outlines of snow-covered mountains, the branches of pines. Light and season invoke mood, plants and animals point beyond physical representation to an inner life and growth. The perspective is calm, but the content is ceaselessly moving. The landscape painting does not rest in a single focal point or in a definite moment, but draws the eye in to its windings and spaces, its valleys and bays, its heights and depths, allowing the mind to wander over the fixed surface without exhausting the scene. The Tao is present in white cloud space, in green tree and river depths, in curving shorelines and falling water, in the shapes of mountains, the bones of the earth, cliffs and gorges, fissures and caverns, erosion and layering, cascades and torrents.

In the Tale of Genji there is an evocative scene. 'The emperor loved to paint which he did beautifully and to look at paintings.' He encourages his ladies to paint and collect. Genji and Murasaki sort out a set of paintings that includes 'moving and interesting pictures of those tragic Chinese ladies Yang Kuei-fei and Wang Chao-chün.' There is a competition between the ladies where illustrations of stories are compared and the stories discussed. The chapter 'A picture contest' culminates with the Emperor viewing selected paintings with Genji acting as umpire. The power, fluidity and gracefulness of the old masters are contrasted with the ingenuity and technical skill of the moderns. Genji's scroll evoking his life at Suma beach wins with its delicacy and sureness of touch. The ability of art to recreate emotion in the audience is key. 'They had pitied him and had thought they had suffered with him, but now they felt how it had actually been. They saw the bleak unnamed shores and bays.' 'He had depicted the mood of those years.'

Wang's mother, who died when he was about fifty-one years old, in 750AD, had been a Buddhist, as were his brothers. At her death he resigned from office and performed a ritual three years of mourning to express his love for her, and acknowledge their Buddhist beliefs. Taoism was a component of Wang's creativity, but his spiritual feelings often seem to be pushing at the boundaries of Taoism. His poems on visiting temples, and on meditation and reclusiveness, among the mountains and the white clouds, point to his Buddhist yearnings to 'pass the Gate' and achieve a deeper state of being. The admixture of Buddhism with Taoism was a potent one within the personal temperaments of many poets and painters, and Wang Wei exemplifies the co-existence and contrast of two profound ways of thought. 'I have come here' writes Genji with a degree of dissembling as he visits the Buddhist Temple, 'to find out whether I am capable of leaving this world. Tranquillity is elusive and isolation grows. There are things I have still to learn.'

Landscape for Old Man Yu on His Birthday, Yuan Jiang (1691 – 1746)

BUDDHISM

Buddha's story is of the young prince Gautama who horrified at the nature of life in the world searches for, and finds, enlightenment and the route to a higher and nobler existence. His sermon in the Deer Park, at Benares in northern India, laid out the core teaching. Buddhism was to be a Middle Path between ascetic self-torture and worldly indulgence. Enlightenment would lead to knowledge, knowledge to calm, calm and meditation to a higher enlightenment, and ultimately to Nirvana, extinction of the self and release from the Hindu Wheel of Rebirth. Buddhism would concentrate on addressing life in this world, and Buddha evaded as inappropriate and inessential the questions of the existence of the soul, or life after death, or the existence of eternal mind. There is an implied atheism and in the *anatta* or 'no-soul' doctrine an implied rejection of the concept of the permanent self, but the focus is on the reality of humankind's life in the world.

The young prince found it to be possessed by impermanence (*anicca*) and illusion (*anatta*), pain and grief (*dukkha*), illness and death. From this world there was a need to escape through transcendence, through detachment, through a way of life that could bring peace. The Deer Park sermon articulated the Four Truths and set turning the Wheel of the Law (*dharma*). Firstly the noble Truth of pain itself: that birth, life, death, sickness, sorrow and despair are pain, everything we grasp is pain. Secondly the noble Truth of the cause of pain: that pain is born out of our craving, our grasping, our desires, the craving for passion, existence, and non-existence that leads to imprisonment in the cycle of rebirths. Thirdly the noble Truth of the cessation of pain: that pain ceases through the abandonment of craving, the extinction of desires, through non-attachment and release from grasping. Fourthly the noble Truth of the Way that leads to cessation: through the path of right behaviour, intention and awareness. These four truths are the essential teaching.

The follower is bound to avoid violence, crime and indulgence. 'Having set aside violence against any creature the follower is ashamed to cause hurt, imbued with kindness, compassionate and benevolent towards all living things. Having set aside what is not given the follower expects only what is given, the Self being pure. Having put away all deceit, the follower lives for truth and reason.' Without caste or discrimination, Buddhism is a way of equality for anyone who wishes to achieve enlightenment. The ultimate end of the Way is Nirvana, the blowing out of the flame of self, the waning away of all suffering. As in Patanjali Yoga its aim is 'the deliberate cessation of the random activity of the mind'. Nirvana is the state that like the Tao cannot be described. It is neither existence nor non-existence in any normal meaning. It is a silence, an illumination, beyond the Wheel of Rebirths. It is a personal route to bliss. 'Decay is a process inherent in all compound things.' said the dying Gautama to his disciple Ananda, 'Seek out your own salvation with diligence.'

One of the early Buddhist psalms says 'I have put aside all desire, for this or for another life, being one who has reached out to truth, who's heart's at peace, who's self is tamed and pure, seeing the world's unending flow.' This is a perception of the Vortex. The mind has 'gone beyond'. Nirvana is like the quenching of a blazing fire, in which the flames of suffering, being, existence, rebirth, and craving are extinguished.

The stream of Buddhism, Theravada (The Way of the Elders), which attempted to stay close to the pure teachings flourished in Burma, Thailand and Shri Lanka. Its hymn is 'Gata, gata, paragata, parasangata, bodhi, swaha', 'Gone, gone, gone beyond, gone altogether beyond, Oh, what an awakening, all hail.' Theravada is the Way of the single one, of renunciation and ultimate extinction of the self in the Void. In its pure form it creates and satisfies a longing for stillness and release, and Nirvana is interpreted as a state of mind empty of all content, ideas, sensations and feelings. It can be achieved through intense concentration causing all craving and attachment to cease. Mindful of Buddha's own teaching there is an inherent paradox in trying to use striving to end striving, and in eliminating the mental world that is the flux and vortex of the only reality. Theravada can be seen as a world-denying doctrine.

The Buddhism that dominated in China and Japan was the Mayahana (Greater Vehicle) school which stressed the incompleteness of that salvation for the self that excluded others, and whose key concept is the Bodhisattva, that is the Buddha who from the verge of Nirvana turns back to save humankind. Mahayana in China, particularly in the form of the Pure

Land School with its Bodhisattva, Amitabha (Amida in Japan), taught a casteless doctrine of non-violence, compassion and loving concern. Alongside it the Ch'an (Zen) or Meditation school developed out of the convergence of Taoism and Buddhism and remained closer to the Theravada doctrine relying on personal enlightenment and illuminating insight. These three strands of Theravada world-denial, Mahayana compassion, and Ch'an illumination of the Vortex as the Void, all contributed to the complexity of Chinese practice.

The ceaseless flow of the Vortex, that is the Tao, is for Ch'an Buddhism the Void whose perception and naming by the mind generates the illusion (*maya*) of a reality, a sea, of discrete entities and events (*samsara*). Reality is beyond concept, and beyond words, and available truly only by a direct pointing, or a moment of illumination. The world in Taoism and Buddhism is essentially ungraspable, elusive, and shadowy. The attempt to grasp, to realise self, is self-defeating. Both ways of thought see morality in terms of equality, compassion, non-violence, and integrity, arising from the innate understanding of the enlightened human being. Though Buddhism codifies its practices in a way that Taoism rejects as unnatural, both discard the inessential that includes all forms of grasping and excessive attachment. They thereby discard what a moral code would regard as crime, immorality, sin, and evil action, as not conducive to achieving the goal.

The Taoist's aim is to relinquish analysis and classification in achieving harmony, spontaneity, tranquillity, simplicity, and elimination of inessential action and thereby realise the Tao. The Buddhist's goal of meditation is to realise a similar non-analytic state that defeats *maya,* the illusion of the myriad creatures, and rests in the Void. It is achieved by the relinquishment of craving, thereby eliminating the self from the cycles of existence.

The element of world-rejection in Theravada Buddhism is alien to Taoism. Buddhism goes beyond the natural world. Taoism seeks to be in harmony with it. Buddhism sees suffering and the Wheel of Rebirth. Taoism sees a natural path without suffering within the world, and never anticipates rebirth. Both ways of thought have however played many variations on the theme, generating a popular Taoism intoxicated with the search for immortality, often through sexual practices or sympathetic magic, and a popular Buddhism of worship of the Bodhisattvas. But the pure forms of Buddhism and Taoism that search for individual enlightenment overlap in their concept of the un-nameability of reality, an approach to it through the rejection of analysis and naming, and a realised state of mind or attitude that results before death, in inner harmony.

Wang Wei often seems to be yearning for a peace and stillness offered by Buddhism that is beyond the harmony with Nature. If the Peach Blossom Spring is his expression of the heart's desire for the Taoist paradisial state of spontaneity and simplicity, the White Clouds that appear as a motif in many of his poems are the Buddhist Gateway to the extinction of the heart's pain. The deaths of his wife and beloved mother lead to long periods of mourning and retreat from the world. Wang may have known of that Ch'an doctrine that identifies the Wheel of Rebirth with the moment to moment existence of the body and mind, so that rebirth continues as long as there is the identity of a Self that renews in every instant. Nirvana is then the cessation of the circling of the mind, the turning about of the spirit, the moving waves of analytical thought, and the disturbances of the body. Nirvana has then the same goal as Yoga.

Wang Wei's yearning was for the realisation of this state, the cessation from all forms of pain, through the abandonment of craving. He would try to 'reign in the dragon' of desire as in his poem *'Visiting the Temple'* [p. 141]. His poem *'Going to the Temple'* [p. 142] describes the ten stages of perception, the progression towards Nirvana. His poems *'Meditation'* [p. 143], *'The Recluse'* [p. 144] and *'From the Mountain'* [p. 145] clearly show his affiliation to the Ch'an School of meditation rather than to the Pure Land School of the Bodhisattvas but both aspects probably claimed his allegiance. The poem *'How Fine'* [p. 155] blends both Taoist and Buddhist perception. Taoism is the harmonious beauty of nature and spontaneous art, outside worldly commitment. Buddhism is the 'empty' Refuge beyond the visible world.

It is clear that Wang Wei's spiritually serious temperament struggled in attempting to relinquish those deep feelings that are obvious in his poems, and that overwhelmed him at the time of his wife's and mother's deaths. As a Confucian trained official he felt a duty to exercise his great talents on behalf of the State, and always returned to State service, though he never occupied the very highest offices. As a Taoist artist he used his Wang River retreat to reconcile himself to Nature, and his poetry, painting and music as a means of cultivating the spirit of concordance with the Vortex. But as he grew older his deepest yearnings may have been for release from the pain and burden of existence. If being in the world is like a hand grasping, and craving like a fist formed by desire and greed, then Nirvana is the opening of the hand, the vanishing of the fist, the disappearance of 'names and forms'.

Ch'an and Taoist thinking merged. In the late T'ang Chinese commentators on the Dharmadatu, the culmination of Indian Mahayana thinking, expressed the view that harmony is achieved when everything is left to be freely and spontaneously itself. There is no conflict or obstruction (*wu ai*) between things and events (*shih*), or between them and their underlying reality (*li*). This Buddhist concept is clearly a restatement of the Tao and the Myriad Creatures, the Vortex, and the continuity of flow. The Vortex is thus also the Void, and Samsara and Nirvana, reality and its extinction, are one when naming and analysis ceases. Again the Six Precepts of Tilopa declare: 'Without mind, without meditation, without analysis, without practice, without the will, let it all be so.' This is the Taoist *tzu-jan*, the 'natural' or 'spontaneous' inner meaning of things and events.

Ch'an Buddhism is 'Beyond any doctrine: apart from all tradition: not based on words or scriptures: a direct pointing at the human mind - seeing into our nature, achieving Nirvana.' Hui-neng (637-713AD) the Sixth and greatest Patriarch of the Ch'an School expressed that sudden pointing that is the awakening (*satori*) of Zen. A humble man he became the successor to Hung-jan the Fifth Patriarch through answering a poem written on the wall by Shen-hsiu.

'The body is the Bodhi Tree, the mind is a bright mirror.' Shen-hsiu's poem ran, 'Clean the mirror, and allow no dust to cling.' Hui-neng's reply pointed instead to the illusion of *maya* and the error of seeing the world as 'names and forms'. 'There is no Bodhi Tree. There is no shining mirror. At root no things exist. How can the dust cling?'

His attitude was to abandon useless meditation, to remove the barriers, to avoid stirring the thoughts. 'Carry water, chop wood'. That was all that 'sitting in meditation' required, involving neither sitting nor meditation. And the Great Void for Hui-neng is the Taoist nameless space-time of sun, moon, earth and stars. The mind is this Void where thoughts and feelings pass like the birds in the sky without leaving a trace.

Energies, particles, within their probability waves, leap, randomly, out of the seething ocean of quantum reality only when they are observed. The Void shines. The Vortex pours. Unobserved reality allows only the potentiality of discrete entities at the quantum level. Particles are neither here nor there. They are everywhere, with some probability or possibility of being. The torrent of energies is also the cloud of particles. *Yun shui*, cloud and water, is a common term for the student of Zen Buddhism, who must wander like a cloud, and flow like water. 'What is the Tao?' asked the Governor of Lang, of Yao-shan. Yao-shan pointed up to the sky, and then down at a dish of water. Asked what he meant, he replied 'Cloud in the sky, water in the dish.'

In Wang Wei, Buddhist and Taoist quietism and the deep love of nature converge. His poems exist in the Void and the Vortex. They point at human life within Nature but without analysis. Their luminous stillness refrains from describing. It declares and evokes. They require a slow attention from the reader. They avoid the demonstrative. They have neither the mature worldly engagement of Tu Fu, nor the brightly lit flickering movement of Li Po. They are Yin to Li's Yang. They are inwardness to match Tu's outwardness. There is a gentle sadness perceptible in his work, so delicately poised that it never becomes negativity. He is the darkness (hsüan) of the Tao, as he portrays himself in a poem *'From the Wang River Scroll'* [p. 159], playing his music in the bamboo grove hidden from all except the Moon. 'There is a thing that holds up the heavens and supports the earth.' says T'ung-shan, 'It is black like lacquer, and it moves continually.'

As the poem *'White Hairs'* [p. 161] says, Wang Wei knew what it was to be 'hurt by life'. He was a man of profound feelings who was able to enter into and use solitude, as he would have used the unpainted silk of the empty background in his paintings. 'Understanding the depths of landscape', he says in *'Pa Pass'* [p. 140] 'even here I am never lonely.' Cold, cloud, thin rain, shadows, water, evening, soft breezes, deep woods, pale light, cool air, peach blossoms and moonlight. This is Wang Wei.

Landscape, Yuan dynasty (1260 – 1368)

EMPEROR HSÜAN-TSUNG

Emperor Hsüan-tsung came to the Imperial T'ang throne in 712 AD, the year of Tu Fu's birth, and his Court was soon the focal point for a high culture. The early years of his reign saw him exercise a tight grip on government. The power of his imperial relatives who had gained from the influence of the Empress Wu was curbed. He ordered a new census, and reformed the equal field system designed to share out the land, a State resource, between families, in order to increase the tax revenues. The aim, when the system had been initiated by the Northern Wei government in 486AD, was to bring all land into cultivation, to provide stability, to prevent monopoly ownership by the rich and powerful, and to ensure that as many families as possible were brought into the taxation system. Taxes were levied in grain and cloth.

The Emperor set up an outer ring of military provinces along the western and northern borders with substantial devolved authority being given to the commanders. Within the strengthened frontiers economic development was rapid, particularly in the south. River transport enabled the tea trade for example to spread throughout the country, turning tea from a medicinal herb to an everyday drink. The southern ports grew to support the extensive sea trade across South-East Asia and along the coastlines. By the middle of the eighth century the previously lightly populated south had as many people living in it as the north.

The Emperor encouraged the codification of State ritual and had a broad-minded interest in philosophy and religion. Teachers of various systems including Buddhism, Taoism, and even the esoteric Tantric Buddhism were welcome at his Court. Elite families still dominated Court circles but leavened with officials who had entered service through the examination system.

Educated men understood Taoism, Buddhism and Confucianism, were drawn to the arts and scholarship, and had the leisure to practice them. Ancient texts were collected and treasured. Poetry was an accomplishment of a gentleman, and every civilised man could turn out a suitable poem on a friend's departure for a journey. While travel was still time-consuming and arduous, and communications difficult, the improved road and canal system with its established post stations and the massive volume of river traffic allowed movement in relative safety. Leisure trips and official duties encouraged a criss-crossing of the vast country.

The political stability of the first thirty years of the reign with war limited to the northern and western borders, peace within the inner Empire, a strengthened code of laws, and rapid economic growth stimulated a brief golden age.

It was a Renaissance in the sense of re-creating the unified vigorous Empire of the Han Dynasty, though a great deal of cultural development had continued in the fragmented Period of Division. Buddhism, Taoism, poetry and painting had all flourished since the Han, and the T'ang was a recipient of this. The T'ang Renaissance could look back towards an earlier Classic civilisation and its great men, and could blend together the three streams of moral and spiritual thought represented by Confucianism, Buddhism and Taoism. There is a flavour of the Florentine Renaissance's stimulus at the re-awakening knowledge of Greece and Rome, and its parallel blending of Christianity, and Classicism with Secular and Pagan cultural streams.

As in the West an emphasis on the golden age can lead to a wrong belief that other periods were times of total cultural darkness. Decentralised fragmentation gave a freedom and variety that was a stimulus to complex development. Just as the intellectual life of the Middle Ages already presaged the Italian, French and English Renaissances, so the periods either side of the T'ang were fruitful in less spectacular ways. Nevertheless T'ang China was a high point. Japanese, Korean and Vietnamese culture benefited from the contact with China. Heian Japan modelled parts of its Court culture on the Chinese example. Chinese poetry, paintings and history were admired and studied. There is a parallel with the adoption of French culture within nineteenth century Russian aristocratic circles.

To promote and sponsor new poetry and calligraphy and provide the Court with a T'ang literature, Hsüan-tsung set up the Han-lin Academy, the 'Forest of Writing Brushes'. The Academy was responsible for example for drafting significant State documents. Distinguished poets joined the Court and celebrated Imperial life in their verses. Li Po arrived in Ch'ang-an in

742 at the age of forty-one to become a member of the group. 'I rode a horse from the Emperor's stables, with silvered stirrups and a jade-studded saddle. I slept in an ivory bed, sat on a mat of silk, ate from golden dishes. People who had once ignored me now came humbly to pay their respects.' Classed amongst the professional men and therefore of relatively lowly status, Li wrote occasional pieces, private poems of drinking and farewell, public poems celebrating the beauty of the Imperial parks, and the ladies of the Court. The 'Three Poems on Wine [p. 170]' are from this time.

Music and dance, song and mime, were also Court arts. There were dance schools in the Spring Gardens and in the Pear Garden inside the Imperial Palace. Tu Fu writes nostalgically about the greatest dancer of the eighth century Lady Kung-sun performing mime and dance steps originating west of the Yangtze. The Taoist ideals of spontaneity, natural flow, concentration of the attuned spirit, and controlled impulsiveness run through the arts. Her fluid and dynamic dance style for example influenced the calligraphic writing of large hanging inscriptions, which demanded similar initial pent-up concentration, fluid style, brilliant attack, and physical agility, its flowing continuity suddenly brought to rest, as Tu Fu says 'like the cold light on a frozen river'. Such calligraphy was compared to whales arching from the sea: snakes winding through tall grass: lashing rain or silk threads blown by the wind: giant creepers hanging from vast cliffs brushing the autumn pools: or black dragons ascending from a darkened ocean into the winding immensities of night.

Sometime in the late 730's after the death of a favourite concubine, which at first left him inconsolable, Hsüan-tsung, who had many consorts, became infatuated with Yang Yü-huan. She was the young wife of one of his sons, beautiful and skilled in music. Now and later he was obsessed, by her and her memory. She became the Favourite Concubine, Yang Kuei-fei. Before her formal entry into the Palace as consort in 745AD she was installed as a Taoist nun in a convent in the Palace grounds.

The Emperor's obsession with her brought her family and favourites power. The Chief Minister Li Lin-fu exercised almost absolute control from now till his death in 752 and the Emperor relinquished government, spending his time in entertainment and extravagance with his beloved concubine, indulging in esoteric and erotic practices that promised immortality, or promoting military campaigns designed to win glory. Li Lin-fu, an uneducated man ran an oppressive regime, his opponents condemned on flimsy charges and done to death by roving executioners. Li Yung a friend of Tu Fu and Li Po was killed in this way through implication in a supposed plot to dethrone the Emperor. Li Po writing of a melancholy visit to Li Yung's former house says 'Even the trees he planted in his life have entered Nirvana, untouched by spring.'

The tenor of the reign had altered from controlled excellence and even austerity to reckless extravagance and political corruption. Increased taxation to fill the revenues and fund the military expeditions was combined with self-serving officials who used influence alone to gain wealth and power. The Confucian ideals were becoming lost. It is not too fanciful to find echoes of Tudor England not only in the cultural Renaissance but also here in the troubled, distracted and oppressive atmosphere at the end of Elizabeth's reign. The Military build-up on the borders, combined with devolved authority vested in non-Chinese generals supposedly without political affiliation, created a dangerous alternative power-base. Equally the costly wars of attrition did not go well. In 751 China suffered two great defeats one in Yünnan to the north and one in distant Turkestan at the battle of the Talas River. In Yünnan the untrained soldiers of the levy were 'frightened human beings not fighting men' and died of malaria like flies. At the Talas River the army was caught between Turkish and Arabic forces and most of the men were lost. The pain of military disaster and war's inhumanity is present in the poetry, in Li Po's *We Fought for - South of The Walls'* [p. 189], in Tu Fu's *'Ballad of the War Wagons'* [p. 199] and *The Homecoming'* [p. 201]. Discontent at the Talas River defeat simmered amongst the generals and in the country at large. Later events, driven partly by this defeat, led to the Chinese abandonment of Central Asia for centuries.

One of these generals was a court favourite. An Lu-shan (703-757AD) had built up considerable forces around the Peking area as Li Po witnessed in 744, perhaps a hundred and fifty thousand troops, and had also established a power base at Court through Yang Kuei-fei. He was a soldier of fortune from Sogdiana descended from a family of Iranian soldiers on his father's side, and with a Turkish mother. Yang Kuei-fei adopted him and made him wealthy, gifting him increased military commands and providing him with horses from the Imperial stables, such that by 744 he had potential control of north eastern China.

After Li Lin-fu's death in 752 ministerial power passed to a distant cousin of Yang Kuei-fei, Yang Kuo-chung. The reign was increasingly unpopular. There was a series of economic disasters in the early 750's including spring droughts, loss of a grain-transport fleet, typhoons that destroyed shipping at Yangkow, severe autumn rains and flooding, and the effects of hurricanes. Food prices rose and the Government released grain at reduced prices but in inadequate quantities. The influence of Yang Kuei-fei, her sisters and her power base on the Emperor and the Empire lead to many poetic references to Han and other precedents. The beautiful concubine who became a consort with undue influence was always a likely consequence of the Imperial system, and there were plenty of examples. Li Po's 'The Roosting Crows [p. 184]' hints at the Taoist sexual practices, aimed at gaining immortality, practised by King Wu and Hsi Shih. Tu Fu's 'By the Waters of Wei' [p. 198] pictures Yang Kuei-fei and her sisters in analogy with Flying Swallow and her Maids of Honour of the Han Dynasty. Cruelty, malice, mockery and danger flicker behind the smiling faces in the South Gardens.

Yang Kuo-chung's government was increasingly resented. Tu Fu describes his journey to his wife and children in late 755, as events moved towards crisis. He left Ch'ang-an on a freezing cold night and passed the hot springs where the Imperial war banners blocked the sky, and where Yang Kuei-fei and the Emperor were warm while everyone else froze. 'From the vermilion gate rose the smell of food and wine, in the road were the corpses of men who froze to death.' Arriving home he found that his little son had died in the harshest of circumstances from lack of food.

River-Crossing in the Spring, Yuan Jiang (1691 – 1746)

THE SEARCH FOR IMMORTALITY

The search for Immortality occupied the thoughts of many followers of Taoist practices not least the Chinese Emperors. At one extreme it displayed itself as an illusory, even debased, pursuit of endless life by physical and sexual means. At the other extreme it was a method of pure meditation designed through breathing and inner concentration to achieve states of 'immortality' akin to the Buddhist mental state of Nirvana. As a desire for immortality in the sense of endless life it was the exact opposite of the Buddhist desire for release from the Wheel of Rebirths and thereby for escape from life and death. As a meditative technique akin to the Yogic method it allowed a convergence of Taoist and Buddhist ideals which illuminated the Ch'an (Zen) schools of Buddhism, though the sixth patriarch Hui-neng specifically warned against substituting the 'rituals' of formal meditation for humble awareness.

The force of the Tao, manifests itself in the Vortex, in the 'forms and names' of Heaven and Earth. There its currents and energies take on masculine (Yang) and feminine (Yin) embodiments. The Emperor, as a divine representative of the Tao on earth, as Man positioned between Heaven and Earth, was responsible for regulating the Cosmic process. He must perform the rituals and practise the disciplines that would create the union of Yang and Yin, the union of Earth and Heaven, and so bring himself and his people into harmony with the Tao. He was the intermediary between Heaven and Earth, who could co-ordinate and balance the forces of Heaven, as they worked in the Earth, and reconcile the claims of both. His Court was therefore a magnet for Taoist diviners, astrologers, magicians, doctors, healers and observers who could assist the process. He was aided by surrounding himself with anything in the environment that could create a conducive and symbolic atmosphere, in which to achieve harmony, whether landscape, music, painting, food, perfumes, clothes, or movement and gesture.

The arts therefore reflected the underlying sexual polarity of the universe. Yang, the masculine polarity, has the attributes of sharpness, brightness, dryness, and clarity. It is active, hot, and positive. It is represented by the Feng or phoenix bird, by the dragon, fire, jade, the summer, the south, vertical lines, waterfalls, tall cliffs, straight pine trees, phallic shaped rocks and forms. The feminine Yin has the attributes of depth, emptiness, wetness, and darkness. It is passive, cool, and negative. It is represented by hollow forms, like vases or open peony flowers, by the wetness of lakes, rivers and pools, and by the cloud shapes of smoke, fungi and coral. It is shown in landscape by cloud-shaped wintry mountains and by misty valleys, by horizontal planes and lines. It is symbolised by the tortoise and intertwined snake of winter, night and the north. The Yin is vulva-shaped, peach-shaped, has the mouth of the open chrysanthemum, is the hollow of bronze vessels, and resides in the beauty of young girls.

The Emperor's task was to create the union of Yin and Yang for which the obvious physical correlative is sexual union, and to bring about the union of Heaven and Earth. Within Chinese art there is great concern to symbolise the marriage of Yin and Yang by bringing their representative elements together. Yang mountains meet Yin valleys. Yin mist can be created from empty white silk by painting Yang cliffs. Dragons and Feng birds fly down to gardens with young girls, open flower-heads, fungi and mosses. Waterfalls dive vertically into horizontal pools. Streams flow among tall pines. And there are paintings of men and women in sexual acts, caring and mutually pleasant, to emphasise harmony and the equality of the sexual polarities in the personal sphere.

The union of Heaven and Earth is symbolised, by the jade Tsung (a square tube representing Earth) and Pi (a holed disc representing Heaven), like the Yoni and Lingam of India. It is shown in ceramics as the gourd-shaped vase, two swollen curves with a narrow waist. There are the carved stands of wood and jade, showing twisted roots (Earth) with random holes and hollows (Heaven), or jade clouds and wooden waves. There is the sign of the Great Ultimate (*t'ai chi*), the interlocking tear-shaped Yin and Yang symbols inside a circular disc, within which smaller discs can be drawn along the diameter in an infinitely deep pattern whose serpent-like inner lines converge on the diameter itself. And there is a complex colour symbolism where the gold, blue, green and black of Heaven are juxtaposed with the silver, crimson, purple and white of Earth. Red is used with blue or green, white with blue or black, gold with silver, giving for example the ubiquitous blue and white or green and white porcelains. Or the colours of Heaven and Earth are intermingled and harmonised in the glazes of Celadon wares. Seasons, colours, trigrams of the 'I Ching', forms and shapes, were all combined to express and aid harmony, union and mediation.

The Cosmic spirit of the Tao charges the forms and processes of Heaven and Earth. It is air with its currents of movement in smoke and clouds, its billows and swirls, or water with its flow, its strands and coils of energy. The Taoist practices that used physical means aimed to gather and enhance personal vital energies in order to achieve 'external immortality' that is indefinitely extended life. These vital energies could in turn be used to fuel meditative practices whose end was the condensing of cosmic energy internally within the furnace of the body through an inner alchemy to create the final elixir. This would allow the achievement of 'internal immortality', through an ultimate tranquillity, in harmony with the Cosmic Tao.

One way to start this process, once the environment itself had been made harmonious through the arts of living, was to gather vital energy through a diet of drugs and essences. These are the substances searched for and ingested by the true Immortals, the *hsien* (sennin). These legendary magicians travel through the skies to the Western Paradise, like shamans, on the backs of storks or cranes. They live deep in the woods, or in caves in the mountains, have mastered the Yin and Yang energies, and are reincarnated at the end of each 'life' or are found never to have died at all. The substances they eat include pine juices angelica, certain roots and fungi, and cinnabar. Cinnabar, sulphide of mercury, can be fired in the inner cauldron, when eaten, to condense the Yang and Yin essences and release the elixir of immortality, just as heating the reddish purple crystalline rock releases the silver flow of mercury. Eating pounded cinnabar crystals, counter-productively however, shortened the lives of many of the Emperors through mercury poisoning.

A second stage of gathering vital energy was to tap into the Yin and Yang energies of the natural world. The Tao gives life to nature and humankind, and cosmic energies are condensed and exhaled in natural process. The rising energies can be portrayed in art in the crackled lacquer panels, in marbled ceramics, wood and stone, in the 'dragon veins' of rock strata and the lines of landscape, and in esoteric calligraphy, cloud, bird, constellation and grass scripts, notations for music and even perfumes. The Yin energies of the earth are breathed out as vapour, mist and cloud, or exuded as moss and fungi. The Yin mists and clouds fall to earth again as Yang rain. On the tops of mountains the adept can absorb Yang energy from the bright Heavens, or drink the dew that falls from the moon. Rain and dew are fluids born of the intercourse of Heaven and Earth, charged with cosmic energy. Emperor Wu of Han built bronze pillars with Yin bowls on their tops to collect the dew condensing from the sky for his elixirs. Cloud fungi are female effluvia from this cosmic intercourse.

The ultimate physical absorption of sexual energy is from the human sexual act itself, and the Taoist adept might employ erotic skills with a partner, mutually absorbing the sexual fluids and juices, to build vital energy. The wealthy man could use concubinage and polygamy to cultivate his sexual activities. The symbolism of sexuality therefore pervades Chinese Imperial art.

The vase or bronze vessel is a symbolic vulva, as is the peach, the peony blossom, the golden lotus, the artemisia leaf, pink shell, or vermilion gate. The male organ has all the conventional phallic representations, but is also alluded to by the horned and whiskered dragon and by the plum branch. The sexual fluids may be symbolised by plum blossom falling onto the green moss, dragon's semen congealed as jade, white dew covering jade steps. The fluids may be caught in vulva shaped Yin cups, made of deer or rhino horn, decorated with dragon shapes. Sexual orgasm is the bursting of clouds and rain, the showering of plum blossom, the dragon swirling among clouds. Si Wang Mu, the Western Goddess, the greatest of sexual adepts, came to King Huai in a dream. Giving herself to him she said 'At dawn I am the morning clouds, at evening the falling rain.'

If exercised caringly and with seriousness, tenderness, and skill these practices were potentially mutually satisfying. However the whole attitude easily led in men to a desire for intercourse exclusively with young girls in the belief that absorbing the fluids from their orgasms would give the greatest sexual energy. Confucians and Buddhists disapproved strongly of the abuse of such women, who were then left to grow old and lonely in household service, or were rejected and abandoned. Equally the meditative Taoists pointed out the potential dangers of self-delusion in taking such a route, particularly since the whole craving for immortality by these means could easily destroy rather than enhance the tranquillity and harmony of the mind and spirit.

It can appear as if these men were merely preying on the girls. That is the feeling a Westerner gets from reading about Genji's relationship with the child Murasaki, tender though it is, she who 'is like the wild carnation wet with the fresh dew'. It becomes easy to understand however the attraction of the elderly Emperor, Hsüan-tsung, to the young Yang Kuei-fei. A clever woman could easily manipulate such a situation.

A further dimension was the practice of the man avoiding orgasm in order to conserve the sexual fluids, while encouraging orgasm in the partner, which could equally lead to an unnatural one-sided and inharmonious relationship.

To the meditative Taoist much of this was irrelevant. The adept began instead by sitting contemplatively in harmonious surroundings, looking quietly at paintings of mist and mountains, or gazing at a garden full of convoluted rocks and green mosses. Or contemplating a carved stone object, say a mountain scene with hermits, trees, and deer, made from lapis lazuli, turquoise or jade. The adept then moved on to breathing exercises similar to Tantric Yoga, aimed at arousing the 'subtle body' of meditative energies. The goal was to harness the stored energies of the mind and body, and combine them ultimately with the cosmic energies to achieve harmony and 'immortality'.

The energies are conceived as circulating between three centres one above the other in the body. The lowest centre is below the navel, the middle centre is behind the solar plexus, and the higher centre is behind the eyes. The fundamental energies, stored by sexual practise or abstinence or otherwise, in the lower centre, the vital energy of the middle centre, and the spiritual energy of the upper centre, are transformed, as cinnabar is transformed in the furnace, to generate the elixir.

The adept initiates regular breathing to arouse the subtle fire of energy that will circulate between the centres. A meditative thought track conceives of the 'subtle body' as a flow from the base of the spine up the back to the head, and down again through the front of the body to the sexual organ and back to the base of the spine. When the breath, the continuous flow of

74

the thought-path, and the energy become one, the spine becomes an ascending track of energies that rise as Yang to fall again as Yin.

The 'inner alchemy' moves and combines the three energies in a series of 'firings' and circulations until the combined energy rises up to the head to join with cosmic energies to create a luminous Sun and Moon of radiance. An essence gathers in the mouth that must be swallowed. This may echo the swallowing of the tongue in Indian practices. The essence congeals to form a seed in the lowest centre. While external breathing ceases, internal breathing continues, the radiance enters the seed and creates the Taoist foetus that breathes cosmically. It becomes a Taoist child that rises to the head and merges with the cosmic energies of the Tao. The Immortal is then 're-born' from the top of the head. There are resonances with Western alchemy in the radiant marriage of the Sun and Moon, and in the transforming energies within the 'crucible'.

The Taoist adept becomes an Immortal, and flies on a stork or crane, or rides a dragon or tiger. The Immortals play in the form of children in the green-gold Western Paradise, eat pine-seeds and fungus, drink rain and dew, and are at one with the cosmic energies of the universe. The Emperor who achieves this becomes the divine mediator between Heaven and Earth, Emperor on Earth and Immortal in Heaven, while remaining in human form between the two realms.

Hsüan-tsung and Yang Kuei-fei may have practised some or all of the sexual techniques, and the ageing Emperor may have eaten the drugs and essences, and sat and meditated in his attempts to become an Immortal. He withdrew increasingly from government into the private realm, perhaps concentrating exclusively on these esoteric methods. It is impossible not to feel a gulf between the intricacies of these difficult and artificial 'rituals' and the great humanity and natural life of the poets. Going back into the world of the T'ang poems and later Sung landscapes is like going back into the woods and mountains, clouds and rivers, into the fresh air and subtle colours, out of the constraining darkness of the Imperial palaces and corridors.

Wang Wei merges his Buddhist quietism with real appreciation of nature and escapes into it as a refuge. Tu Fu is moved by landscape as it illuminates the Confucian predicament, the man of integrity floating free in a world of error and confusion. Li Po is also a poet of freedom, in his case of total freedom, but strangely perhaps Li went closest to following the ritualistic practices of the Taoist adepts, fitfully and erratically, alongside his attempts at meditation through the study of Ch'an Buddhism. He was attracted to esoteric Taoism by its magical aspects, by its promise of immortality and Paradise, and by its charm and enchantments. Perversely Li, the least dedicated to public life and also the least conformist of the three poets, might best have understood the position of the ageing Emperor. The representative of Heaven on Earth practised the rites, and chased Immortality, in order to fulfil his role for his people. He who, like Genji, 'held such a position in life that freedom of action was not allowed him.'

Landscape, Zhang Ruitu （1570 － 1641）

THE TAO AND WESTERN SCIENCE

The Tao is the unknowable. 'The bright Way seems dull. The Way up to it seems the Way down.' says the Tao Te Ching. 'The greatest shadow is formless. The Way vanishes in having no name.' The Tao in Western terminology is Energy and the Matrix of energies, the 'stuff' of the Universe and its transformations. It is the microcosmic Vortex and the macrocosmic Void. Its manifestations are the metamorphoses of Energy in detectable forms and processes, the 'myriad creatures' that we name. Paradoxically the brilliant theories and experiments of Western science as they clarify the knowable also reveal the silence of the unknowable.

To separate a cause from its effects, or an object from its surroundings, or a thought from thinking 'creates' the cause and the effect, 'creates' the boundaries of the object, 'creates' the fully formed thought out of the stream of thinking. The chair we touch is not the chair we see. The 'touched' chair is not the 'seen' chair. We assemble and link these views of the chair in our mind. Every 'cause' is itself a nexus of causes and effects, a whirlpool. We select the boundaries of causes and effects to map onto our boundaries of objects and processes. The expressed thought itself is an encapsulation in some language, even a physical or artistic 'language', pulled out of the thought continuum. Its unexpressed tentacles stretch out into surrounding thoughts and language. The word echoes amongst other words. The verbal reaches into the non-verbal.

When we defocus for a moment from our delineated worlds of known boundaries, clear causes, and agreed language, we can easily find ourselves at a loss. In the physical world we are disturbed by discontinuities, 'noise', the non-repeating patterns of water and clouds, dust and smoke, fire and light. The vortices of the world are also the 'weather' of the Universe. The boundaries of the world are fractal boundaries: as in Zeno's paradox they are finite in space but immeasurable. Complex movement is fluid, elusive, evasive, subtle. It creates forms out of nothing and collapses them again. The tiniest effect, the smallest perturbation, may cause massive change. Nature repeats, but not exactly, traces endless paths but within bounds.

The quantum model implies not merely that the future of the world is unpredictable because we cannot compute its changes fast enough, but that it is *intrinsically* unpredictable. Within the 'whole' of Nature are domains where uncertainty and randomness are inherent, where repetition is bounded but non-repeating, where levels of detail regress infinitely. The random, the uncertain, the infinite, and the vastly complex, conspire to make our universe personally ungraspable, despite those domains of our intelligence where we have created theories, demonstrated regularities, inferred 'laws', and built ourselves a world we can grasp. What we can predict at the statistical level escapes us at the level of 'reality'. The 'thing-in-itself' is beyond us. In that sense, since it is ungraspable, there is no 'thing-in-itself'.

In our relativistic universe, moving objects, and objects in gravitational fields have their own 'local' time, dimensions, and energy. Our 'local' perception of them depends on information, such as light signals. When we perceive them their clocks run slower than ours, as ours do to them. Dimensions contract. Mass, which is Energy, increases. The results of what we measure will depend on relative velocities, on gravitational fields, on inertial effects. The 'observer', the point from which we observe, becomes crucial. Not because the key 'laws' of physics run differently in different domains but because each observer, each different set of observers, each domain, sees a different universe. Subtly, or in some situations radically different. We can navigate 'our' universe, but we cannot see and touch 'the Universe' directly, or see it whole. We can imagine and visualise it relativistically. We can construct diagrams and model it mathematically. But we cannot, ever, 'grasp it' entire. That there is a universal 'Now' how can we doubt? But it is intrinsically not observable as a single 'state of everything'. There is no absolute framework from which to observe it. The stone dropped from the railway carriage window appears to drop vertically to the passenger in the moving train, but describes a parabola to the watcher on the embankment. Which path does it 'really' follow. That is a Zen *koan*. Meditation on it brings illumination.

Events that happen simultaneously for one observer, can happen sequentially for another distant observer, because of the difference in the length of the paths the information travelled to reach that distant observer. There is no universal simultaneity of observations, no universal 'Now'. That is a second Zen koan. Meditation on a koan creates first confusion and frustration, then enlightenment. 'At first' said Ch'ing-yüan 'I thought that mountains were mountains and rivers were rivers. Later, on considering these things, I realised that mountains were not mountains and rivers were not rivers. Eventually I achieved enlightenment. I came to understand that mountains are mountains, and rivers are rivers.'

In our quantum universe the sub-atomic world is strange. There is no satisfactory visual model of the entities or continua that make up the microcosm. They appear and vanish. They carry with them a cloud of other entities. They seethe in a sea of reality that appears only in observation. The statistically predictable pattern is made up of intrinsically unpredictable events. The uncertainty principle prevents knowledge of the precise 'state' of the universe. In measuring one attribute we destroy information about another. No sub-atomic entity can be observed twice. What is observed is always a different entity. All events are unique. Randomness is at the core of the microcosm. Only statistical prediction is valid. The observer changes the observation and is a crucial part of the observation. The 'particle' that 'must' go through one hole in the two-slit experiment appears at the screen having 'travelled' as a probability 'wave' through both holes. The pattern of the interference fringes dictates where the particle can appear on the screen. Its precise location is probabilistic and unpredictable. Is it 'really' a particle or is it 'really' a probability wave? This experiment is also a Zen koan. Enlightenment 'realises' what is strange. It 'finds the sun inside the rain, draws water from the roots of fire'.

The world of our mental processes is also impenetrable to self-reflection. The conscious mind cannot 'see' its own subconscious processes. The sources of our feelings, motivations and affinities are therefore not totally knowable. We absolutely have no language for feelings other than the language of how they affect others and the world. What does a 'feeling-in-itself' feel like? I know but cannot tell. I only hope you also know. We try to evoke the feeling through art, through action, through the spaces between words. Emotion and sensibility create image and situation so that image and situation may in turn re-create sensibility and emotion. We conjure in order to communicate, between the islands of our selves. The mind is a hand that cannot grasp itself, a mirror that cannot reflect itself, a process in time that can never be an object in space. 'You will not grasp it by thinking about it. You cannot realise it without thinking about it.' says Zen, of enlightenment. And again 'What is the meaning of Reality? Wait until there is no one around and I can tell you.'

Even Time is elusive and ungraspable. Our local time is created locally by the movement from one configuration to another configuration, from one set of events to another set of events, of the energies that make up our local universe. How can there not be a local 'Now' where events occur? We measure time through regularity, through recurring 'identical' oscillations. We agree to meet at a local time, at a distance from 'Now' just as we agree to meet at a local place, at a distance from 'Here' and amazingly we do meet. For us time 'flows' in a direction because events succeed one another. Configurations and events including our eye-movements and thoughts appear in a specific order. Yet there is still only the 'Now'. Neither past nor future exist. The past configuration is not here. The future configuration is not here either. Yet past events 'must have happened'. We infer them from cause and effect. We remember them in the mind. They have left their traces 'bound in' as information and configuration in the present. Future events 'will happen' because their macrocosmic causes are visible in the present.

Relativity theory says that since time intervals can differ at different speeds for different observers then one observer can age more slowly than another does. There is no universal 'Now' only local ones. In this sense there could be time travel into another's future. We could leave and then revisit our society's 'Now' when less of our years and more of its years would have gone by. We would have re-entered the 'Now' of our society without having experienced its intervening moments, like the sleeper waking. Though it would be profoundly strange it would not be travel into our own personal future. Our own personal future is always not here, not yet. It is always ungraspable.

Could we travel into the past, and so get back to a previous configuration? By that would we mean that all processes would continuously backtrack, undo and reverse themselves to a previous 'Now' and 'Here'? Then we would still perceive that reversal appearing in order in forward time. The film that is run backward still runs in our forward flow of time, even if what it shows is a reversing process. Each reversed moment of the physical past, would be a new 'Now' from which a forward future would insist on unfolding. So our perceived time would still run in the one direction. The future is not of the same kind as the past. The future is always possible. The past is always consumed. Every new configuration is the next moment. Every past configuration is no longer a moment.

How could the processes be reversed? The universe has no intention, no will to initiate such a reversal, and no universal information about the totality of its past configurations. We perceive processes that achieve disorder from order, irretrievably dissipating energy in the process. We perceive other processes that achieve order from disorder requiring energy in the process. Disorder stays disordered unless energy is added to create order. One type of process is reversed by the other type of process. Even if the mathematical model looks the same 'with a reverse of sign', losing energy is not the same as adding energy. We can feel that deep in ourselves. Order is not merely disorder reversing. Order 'decays' into disorder but is 'created' from disorder.

And if the 'Now' did in some sense reverse to a previous state there would be no way of knowing it had done so completely since complete description of the 'Now' is denied us by quantum uncertainty and 'infinite' complexity. If the universe must contain microcosmic events that are random and unique then reverse processes must also contain events that are random and unique. Each process is ultimately unknowable in precise, deterministic terms. If we attempted to reverse the process we could not achieve an exact reversal. The process of reversal would itself introduce new and unique random events into the unknowable local universe.

By travel into the past could we mean that a previous configuration of the universe or the total information about it might exist 'somewhere' unchanging in a 'parallel (that is orthogonal) universe' so allowing us to enter it and participate in it? But that past would then not be past but a 'parallel Now', frozen 'alongside' this Universe. There would be an infinite number of parallel 'Nows'. What could it mean to say that a frozen universe exists in another 'Now' alongside this Universe? Nothing is frozen, everything unfolds. If the Universe has infinite dimensions then all 'Nows' are within it. And for the observer there can only be one local 'Here' and 'Now'.

There is no 'memory', in the energies outside us, of the past configurations of even this Universe. The Universe is without mind. We are the minds. There is no universal Will that might control. The Universe is neutral. The Tao of Energy is 'without possession, without demands, without authority.' 'The moon does not intend to create its reflection in the water, the water does not intend to reveal the reflection of the moon.' And neither of them has any mind to be observed by us.

The Universe and the Tao are ultimately unknowable, in the West as in the East. Who observes is crucial. Partial and local 'observations' of events are available to us, and available more or less precisely, but absolute and universal observation of 'all' events with deterministic precision is *intrinsically* impossible. The position of 'the observer' and the observed is crucial in the relativistic universe because the measured 'reality' depends on relative location and velocity, and the presence of gravitational fields. The intervention of the 'observer' is crucial in the quantum universe because measurement 'disturbs' and in a sense 'creates' the 'reality' that is measured, while the uncertainty principle denies complete knowledge. The perspective of the 'observer' is crucial in the chaotic universe because different levels of the fractal infinities within finite 'reality' are visible dependent on scale. And the 'observer's' unconscious processes are crucial in events within the mind because they are the invisible substratum that is part of 'thinking'. Without the observer there is no reality. And each reality is local, uncertain, partial, and scaleable. The space-time of modern science is not smooth but coarse. The surface is 'really' a sea of waves and ripples, swirls and vortices, foam and spume. Instead of a continuum there is a labyrinthine network of cavities and folds, surfaces and holes. The deepest insight is to 'see' that in the quantum universe every part is connected to every other part in a vast, indivisible Vortex, that is a Void without reality until we separate observations from it, creating 'names and forms'. Science makes theoretical models of great empirical power that are still models and not the reality. Heisenberg said that the mathematics describes what we know of the universe's behaviour not the behaviour itself. Bohr said that science concerns what we can say about Nature not what it is. Sub-atomic entities have no meaningful existence or properties except as we perceive them in observation.

The 'real' mirror is empty. The universe that exists beneath, beside, beyond our observations and our names is visible to us as, at best, a shadow, or a brilliance. Within it there are no names and no forms. 'At root there are no things.' That is why the universal Tao is nameless, and the eternal Way cannot be told. The Tao is the unknowable matrix of energies. It creates the Vortex of the visible and named. It is the Void of the invisible and unnamed. The reality is that we cannot escape the 'observer', cannot escape ourselves. In order to live with the 'observer', live with ourselves, we can only attempt to know the unknowable, be in harmony with the non-existent. That means that we must embrace the non-analytic, non-verbal emptiness, and vanish into the Vortex. What cannot be understood, what cannot be measured, what cannot be analysed, what cannot be grasped, can still be lived. The Universe does not understand the mathematical equations of its own existence. 'Entering the wild' says a Master about the enlightened ones 'the grass does not move. Entering the river, the water is not stirred.'

Lofty Peak and Dense Woods, Gong Xian (1656 – 1682)

LI PO

Li Po [p. 163] the elusive and fascinating. Li who is like Mozart. The precocious talent, the deeply serious artist, the effortless creator, the romanticist in perfect control blended with the effervescent personality of a Taoist 'child'. There is the same social 'irresponsibility' combined with intense artistic responsibility, spontaneity and creative perfection. There is the same need for freedom, resentment of authority, disdain for accepted forms and constraints. The same enchantment with magical rituals (The Magic Flute and Freemasonry parallel esoteric Taoism and Buddhism) and the colours of what is most alive. There is the same deep sensitivity and aesthetic subtlety combined with tensile strength and sexual vigour. There is the same ability to play every note of the scale, from the powerful and masculine to the tender and feminine. There is the same susceptibility to drink, 'entertainment', and pretty women as a means to release creative tension, escape constraint, and achieve spontaneity. The same inability to hold an official post for long. The same generosity, or carelessness about money, so that it flows through his fingers. The same roaming between cities, and wandering between lodgings. The same consciousness of and pride in his own genius. Underlying everything the same deep humanity. The same fluidity, the same enigmatic invisibility behind, or rather transparency in front of, his creations.

Sometimes he appears to be nothing more than his creations. That is the achievement of harmony. Not through meditation, but through being. Li does not seek or require 'approval'. Social commitment and integration are irrelevant to the Tao. Equally humanity, empathy, sensitivity are deep components of his Taoist awareness. Li is the essentially lovable, gifted human being who challenges the leaden conventionality of society, and in some respects is punished for it, by a self-created isolation, through the inability of the world to understand inspiration or achieve the artist's paradise of a continuous and genuinely creative endeavour.

Like a child, like Mozart, he can betray a child's faults and a child's emotional and behavioural extremism. He could be hostile and then overly generous, proud, boastful and then subdued, irresponsible and then deeply serious, rude and then sensitive. It is easy to condemn such a personality as immature or over-sensitive, as egocentric or rebellious. It is equally easy for the artist to react with irony or indifference, pride or disdain, to devalue others efforts, to attack as a means of defence, to ignore as a means of self-protection, to be 'irresponsible' to hide deep hurt. Like Mozart, he is in his art both romantic and classical, concerned with form but aspiring to a world that is more than this world, more satisfying, more beautiful, and more harmonious.

If the pliant, bowing and modest bamboo represents Confucianism, and the scented solitary ancient pine-tree represents meditative Buddhism, it is the plum-bough that represents Taoism. It is the tree of winter whose blossoms burst from the branch, whose sexual essence is the life and sadness of the transient world, whose flowering is spontaneous and free, whose roots are deep and resilient, but whose beauty is evanescent and delicate. Li is the sparkle on the water, the moonlight on the leaf, the flashes of light that contemporaries claimed to see in his eyes, the wild, unkempt, energised lightning of nature.

Li was born in the west of China, possibly over the border in Turkestan. Family traditions claimed descent from Li Kao who created his local dynasty centred on Tun-huang the gate to the Silk Road. The T'ang Emperors claimed the same line of descent and that enabled Li to address the Imperial family as though they were distant cousins. Li Kao was himself a descendant of General Li Kuang (d. 119BC). Ssu-ma-Ch'ien, the great Han Dynasty biographer, brilliantly relates Li Kuang's story in his *Shih chi*, or Records of the Grand Historian. Li Kuang is an archetype of the honest, unassuming, courageous, but unlucky military man. He was named the 'Flying General' by the Huns, the Hsiung-nu, and fought more than seventy actions against them, his successes and failures sadly cancelling each other out, so that he never achieved high honours. Though judged too old he fought a last campaign, taking the blame for a failure to carry out the questionable orders of his superior Wei Ch'ing. Committing suicide, he was mourned throughout the Empire for his integrity, his courage and the sincerity of his intentions. A famous archer with the crossbow, Li Kuang gave rise to a Zenist anecdote illustrating the power of Taoist spontaneity and harmony. Mistaking a rock in the long grass for a tiger he was said to have pierced it effortlessly with an arrow. Trying to repeat the feat consciously he failed.

Li Po's 'Turkish' ancestry provided an exotic element to the self-image that appears in his poetry, and perhaps made him particularly receptive to the Persian and Central Asian influences on Chinese culture. The family history suggests that a later ancestor was in fact banished to the far west around Lop Nor, and drifted further west still. Li Po's father returned to China when Li was a small child, and he was brought up in the southwest, in Szechwan, some distance from the local capital Ch'êng-tu. He was precocious. 'Already, at fourteen, I was reading strange books and writing verse to rival the masters.' 'Already I was seeking the favour of great men.'

As a young man he lived for a time as a Taoist recluse, with a Master, somewhere in the western mountains. 'For several years I never went near a town, and the wild birds ate from my hand without fear. The Kuang-han governor came to see us, offering to send us to the capital as persons of unusual ability but we refused.' It is the image of the adolescent Yeats climbing up to his cave above the sea, or sleeping among the rhododendrons and rocks, playing at being a sage, wizard or poet. It is a young Alastor-like Shelley meditating among the ruins of Rome or making poetry by the Italian seashore. And Li became a *hsieh*, a swordsman, one of those commissioned to seek revenge on behalf of people who could not gain redress. He wandered away from Szechwan and then across eastern China, perhaps supported by relatives, many of them wealthy officials. He certainly scattered money freely.

He also met the great Taoist Master Ssu-ma Ch'êng-cheng, and the desire is visible, that imbues many of his later poems, for spirit journeys into the realms of the Immortals. It aligns him with the shamanistic traditions of ancient China, and with the poetry of the dream-state in East and West. Dream, drink, meditation, immersion in natural beauty, and aesthetic sensitivity were all ways to free the mind and 'fly' through the inner space-time of the creative imagination. Li was capable of composing poetry as Mozart composed music, fluently and spontaneously, with a speed and facility that amazed his contemporaries. Genius can manifest itself as an almost magical flow, an innate harmony with the Tao. Li's qualities were said to be the spontaneity (*tzu-jan*) of natural forces and energies, and the life-breath (*ch'i*) of the deep psyche.

When he was about twenty-five Li made the first of his four marriages to a granddaughter of a former Chief Minister. He lived in Hankow at his wife's family home, seeking recommendations, now and then, for official employment but basically unemployed and remote from the capital. At this time he studied Ch'an Buddhism, practising Dhyana (meditation) 'with a white-eyebrowed monk' at Ju-ning not far from his wife's home, achieving the stage of enlightenment of 'The Wind Wheel Samadhi' where the mind can wander through space. To Li this was no doubt an analogue of the Taoist shamanistic spirit journey that was a determinant of his creative imagination.

He made friends with Mêng Hao-jan who also knew Wang Wei. Mêng was a much-admired poet, with a Taoist indifference to office, and a sensitive love of the elusive 'dream' world reached through drink or natural beauty. Li's poem to him celebrates Mêng's fragrant closeness to the Tao, and Wang Wei's wistful tribute nevertheless points up the Buddhist void that Meng's poetry touched on. One of his poems that influenced Li's poem 'Wine' shows a subtle parallelism, and sensitivity to the free energies and transient forms of the Tao, in storm winds, 'random' birdsong, the chance patterns of fallen blossom, and in the contrasts of sound and silence. The Vortex is all these things. Life is a dream whose contents evade us. Time past scatters round us the results of our dreaming. 'In Spring asleep, lost to morning.' he writes 'wake, hearing, everywhere, birds singing. Through Night's deeps what storm winds sounded. Now, petals, who knows how many, grounded.'

Li already exhibits characteristics of the Taoist attitude. Though Confucian values influence him, he is an individual rather than a social conformist. He respects personal friendship before community. He recognises the ephemeral and transient rather than the permanent. He is for sensitivity not power, beauty not dominance. He is fascinated by the magical though he is conscious of the mundane. He loves personal freedom rather than artificial constraint. He inhabits the elusiveness, and purity of Nature. His mind responds to the deep and the feminine. He loses himself in the dream and the song. Bashō, the great Japanese *haiku* poet, talks about those who have achieved excellence in art being in harmony with nature. 'Whatever they see is a flower, and whatever they dream is the moon. Only a mind without sensibility cannot see the flower. Only a mind without refinement does not dream the moon.'

The flavour of Li's life in his thirties is captured in *The Exile's Letter* [p. 179] that finds him travelling to, and living in, the north perhaps soon after his first wife's early death. He drifted to Shantung where he knew three scholars who lived as recluses by the Bamboo Stream. In 738 he was in Yangchow. In 742, aged forty-one he climbed T'ai-shan the sacred mountain of eastern China. He described ascending it, also, in imagination, riding a white deer, and meeting the faery maidens who smiled and stretched their hands out to him, offering him liquid mist that he was not adept enough to accept. He received writings he could not read, in bird-track script, falling from Immortals concealed in the clouds. And he was mocked, by a child, dressed in green, because of his age and lack of Tao. It is Li growing older, conscious of a yearning he has not satisfied.

At this time he befriended Wu Yün, the Taoist and writer, who was at the Court early in 743, as Taoism gained Imperial favour. Either Wu or the Emperor's sister Yü-chên recommended Li Po for a post, and so Li in his forties joined the Han-lin Academicians as a Court poet. Belatedly he had arrived in Ch'ang-an, where he felt he belonged. Yet he had never deigned to enter for the Civil Service examinations, as Wang Wei, Tu Fu and Mêng Hao-jan had. Had he feared failure, resented conformity, felt himself a 'free spirit' or a genius making his own rules, or did he perhaps know he could never fit in to the sober rigidity of the Civil Service? He remained a 'person in plain dress' as a result, and never achieved high social status. But then neither did Mozart who also longed for a Court post, remuneration, and social recognition. Li stayed as a 'Lost Immortal', a stray genius banished to and confined on earth, one of those creative minds that are loved and recognised in their own domain, but looked askance at in worldly terms. The drunken, 'irresponsible' Li only too conscious of what he believed his own talents deserved prevented the profound, brilliant Li from achieving that recognition He spoke of himself later as an unsuccessful seeker after some position where he could be of influence and utilise his talents.

From his time at Ch'ang-an come the *Three Poems on Wine* [p. 170] in which feelings of isolation, sadness, and yearning are expressed. It is the mood of silence, moonlight, fallen flowers, the mystery and depth of the unknowable universe, the strangeness of life, and its incommunicable essence. Transience, Nature, the Void, the pain of consciousness and the joy of escaping consciousness in natural harmony, being drunk on nature, and in nature, are his subjects. This is the Li of lightness, loneliness, sadness, soft quizzicality, even ironic self-mockery. The same mood is caught in 'Waking from Drunken Sleep on a Spring Day' [p. 174], and 'Drinking in the Mountains' [p. 175]. With gentle, slender touches he creates reflective depth where a subtle and remote troubling disturbs the mirror's surface. Like Mozart he creates harmony and then disturbs it with dissonance. Death and transience are present below the surface of the pastoral. *Et in Arcadia ego.*

He wrote poems at Ch'ang-an which express desire for escape. Perhaps a pose, perhaps frustration at his talents not being properly applied, perhaps an inability to settle into the rigid framework of the Court, and amongst those he considered inferior to himself. He wanted to follow the clouds, vanish into the mountains, see the blossom overhanging the waters, fly with the wild geese. Within a couple of years he was gone, departing around the time in 744 when Yang Kuei-fei was establishing her position at Court prior to her becoming consort. Li fell foul of Chang Chi son of an ex Chief Minister, perhaps through indiscretion and a fondness for drink that did not directly affect his work but made him a risk in terms of official position, leading others to believe he might be unreliable or outspoken. Chang Chi is reputed to have cancelled a promised appointment for Li as a member of the Civil Service. Li's Taoism was also a source of friction with the Buddhist and Confucian trained inner circles. But deeper than that is the temperamental restlessness that he struggles to contain. He achieves peace with himself only with great difficulty. His poems display a yearning for states of illumination and tranquillity that he himself has not attained. He looks with longing at the state of grace that others have reached and knows that a component of his own personality will always prevent the spiritual journey being an easy one. There is sadness and self-irony in his attempts to escape the earthbound reality through drink, or suppress the self in stupor. Poems like 'Lu Mountain [p. 185]', 'Reaching the Hermitage' [p. 187], and 'Hard Journey' [p. 188] are expressions of an internally rather than an externally imposed inability to rest. 'I set off by myself into the deep mountains.' said Bashō, 'White cloud layers lay across the peaks and the valleys were full of the smoking mist and rain.' Li Po understood what Bashō felt at being 'tempted by the wind that blows the clouds, filling me with the desire to wander.' 'He knew again' says the Tale of Genji, 'how hostile the world could become.'

Leaving Ch'ang-an, his hopes dashed, angry at the humiliation of his perceived waste of his time and talent, portraying himself in an Asiatic manner as a caged tiger or a tethered hawk, he knew that time was slipping by and the chances of an official career were becoming remote. He wandered for a while before heading north-eastwards. He reached Peking where he saw An Lu-shan's massed troops, a sign of the gathering power available to a frontier General who was also to become a Court favourite. Soon travelling south again he headed for Honan and there first met Tu Fu, still a young unknown poet, eleven years Li's junior. Tu Fu had attempted the Civil Service examination but failed, and would later try again. He admired the famous Li, and despite the difference in their personalities, the sober and committed Tu Fu no doubt recognised Li's spiritual yearning and the sensitivity that gave Li pain.

At Ch'ang-an perhaps Li had made a second marriage that soon broke up. He now married for a third time to a lady from Lu (Shantung), and they had several children who Li writes about with affection. It is not clear whether the two children from his first marriage survived. He made a home, in Shantung perhaps where his new wife's family lived. Here he went through the Taoist religious ceremony of purification at the Lao Tzu temple at Chi-nan Fu, and received a Taoist diploma, a piece of exquisite calligraphy, as a token of his stage of knowledge, and as a talisman. Tu Fu had a brother in Shantung and met Li again before leaving for Ch'ang-an to attempt the examination. Tu Fu wrote poems about or to Li over the next few years of which *To Li Po'*[p. 208] is a simple example.

The years of Li's late forties and early fifties were years of further wandering and poetic production. He never seemed able to settle with a family, or in any one place, for long, perhaps because he was always seeking a position or being financed by relatives, perhaps because he was constitutionally unable to find satisfaction in home life. He travelled now around eastern China, living for a time near Kaifeng in Honan, with occasional visits to Shantung, and also at Hsüan-chou (Suancheng in Anhwei), Yangchow and Nanking. He finally paused at Ch'ih-chou on the Yangtze south west of Nanking in about 754. During this period he studied Taoist alchemy based on the ancient text the Ts'an Tung Ch'i. Once again there is the yearning for the Taoist paradise, to touch the sun and moon and fuse with the elemental Tao. Perhaps he hoped to become an adept, one of the Fang Shih, or Masters of the Formulae of the Kun Lun sect who drew heavily on the Tantric magic of Buddhism, imported from Tibet. One poem, that draws together alchemy, the wild scenery of the mountains, and the sensation of a spirit journey, describes a vision of the Faerie Goddess in her mountain Paradise. The poem is a *yüeh-fu*, a reworking of an old ballad or folksong form, allowing irregular line lengths, and freer metres. In it Li once more dreams of a place outside the demands of formal life, where he can display his 'true face'. 'At night I flew over Mirror lake', he writes, 'the moon on the water chased my shadow'. Reaching the high mountains, lost amongst the wild flowers, he leans on a rock as darkness falls. Then in a sudden storm lightning splits the peaks, and reveals a fathomless space. 'Over the blue Void's groundless deep, moon and sun fuse silver and gold, Cloud Princesses slant down the air, with Rainbow skirt and misted cloak. White-tigress lutes strike crystal sounds. Drawn by Phoenix birds' flying traces, Heaven's Queen spans the magic spaces, the faerie fields all full of folk.' But his vision once more forces a return to the normal world. 'My mind was stunned, my senses shaken, dazzled by light I cried out loud, and wake to find the empty pillows. All things vanish in mist and cloud.'

Li Po is forever the Chuang Chou of his *'Old Poem'* [p. 176] who is caught between dream and dream, the Taoist dream and the dream of life. His Taoist poems are not merely playing with a graceful mythology of exciting imagery, but like Keats's 'Belle Dame sans Merci' and vanishing nightingale, they are an expression of a deep unrest, an unrequited yearning that is beyond the physical and could never be satisfied within the physical. In that sense, in the restricted sense of his affinity with Keats, Li Po is a 'Romantic'. There is a sweetness there of sensibility. Where Coleridge's 'Kubla Khan' is a vision of an (opiate) Paradise lost, and Shelley's visionary poetry is an attempted, often repeated, assault on the unknowable, Keats and Li Po yearn for something glimpsed but never achieved, a veil that can never be touched or lifted. Reality is a transience that cannot be frozen, captured, held, possessed, or ever fully comprehended. It is a 'bright star'.

Li at this time was described as having 'the flashing eyes of a hungry tiger'. He sometimes wore the green silk hood of the Taoist initiate. His true friends are 'mountains and rivers, moonlight and clouds'. By 756 he was no longer with his third wife. Presumably she and his children remained in Shantung, perhaps at her family home near Sha-ch'iu, nor far from the Tortoise Mountain. He married again, into the Tsung family. At Ch'ih-Chou he saw himself not as the 'Great Roc' of his youth, or the caged falcon, or the quiescent tiger, but as an ageing human being who in his own eyes had failed to realise his dreams.

He stares into Time's glass. 'My white hairs have grown so long. Thirty thousand feet of grieving. In my bright mirror, I cannot understand. Where does it come from all this autumn frost?' In 755 he sent a letter on behalf of the Governer of Hsuan-chou to the Chief Minister Yang Kuo-chung, which thanked him for previous favours and hinted that the Governor, Chao Yüeh would like a position at Court. Perhaps Li also hoped that if Chao succeeded he might still have a chance himself of a post. But this was the eve of the An Lu-shan rebellion, and the Empire was about to be thrown into confusion.

Dream Journey among Rivers and Mountains, Cheng Zhengkui (1604 – 1676)

CONFUCIANISM

In theory Confucian ideals guided the Emperor and his government. While Taoism and Buddhism inspired personal and cultural goals, the influence of Confucius was core to public life. Confucius (K'ung Fu Tzu) was born in 551BC in Shantung during the Spring and Autumn period of the Chou Dynasty. A complex and subtle man, his character and sayings, captured in The Analects, exemplify the life of virtue. He showed sincerity and modesty, courage and conscientiousness, based on restraint and respect. 'In your personal life be courteous, in business be serious, with everyone be sincere.'

Above all he exemplified practical morality, avoiding extremes and rigidity, with humour and wit. Confucian virtue is the fitting of the individual into the social order while benefiting society and the self. At the heart of his practical wisdom was the education of society from the powerful to the powerless without class distinctions. Character was the essential starting point for a well-run state or country. 'The moral character of those who control events is the breeze' he said, 'the character of others is the grass. When the grass feels the breeze it bends.' The state depends critically on the qualities of its leaders.

Taoism takes a route towards the personal life in a world where external forces are neutral. Confucius stressed a life inside the social order in a fundamentally benevolent universe. Taoists poked fun at Confucians blown here and there by the social disasters of warring states and unstable Empire. Nevertheless a life lived according to Confucian ideals could still be informed by Taoist cultural influences and sensitivities. Tu Fu illustrates the Confucian whose poetry is sensitive to a Taoist view of nature and natural harmony.

Confucius successfully ran a transforming government in Lu State, but left when Duke Ting was corrupted. He turned to Wei where he was obstructed by Nan-tzu the wanton, beautiful wife of the Duke whom he had to accompany in her carriage. 'Lust in front, virtue behind' was the people's comment. He journeyed from State to State, 'looking like a dog of an impoverished family', 'a man who knows he can't succeed but who goes on trying'. To the Taoists it showed the worthlessness of public life. To Confucius it revealed the magnitude of the task. Confucius returned to Lu at the age of sixty-eight. But 'Lu failed to employ him, and he no longer wished for office'. He lived quietly, arranging the Classic texts, studying the I Ching. He died at his family home in Shantung. 'He is the sun and the moon that cannot be surpassed' said Tzu Kung.

Confucius stressed the idea of *jen*, benevolence or human empathy, a mutual relationship of sincerity and respect, a total integrity that demands simplicity and reticence, courage and loyalty. 'Do not do to others' he said 'what you would not wish them to do to you'. Integrity was a precursor to proper behaviour or *li*. By integrity and proper behaviour a state could be governed. The duty of a decent human being was to preserve a right relationship to others. Life needed energy and a positive approach but also balance, moderation, and the avoidance of extremes. It is a middle way based on benevolence and justice, wisdom and propriety.

To a true Confucian an Empire at whose heart was an Emperor and his concubines seeking immortality through esoteric practices was an anathema. While the Taoists considered that the Confucians had placed convention and moral rules ahead of harmony, spontaneity and self-cultivation, Confucians considered that both esoteric and non-esoteric Taoism potentially undermined the social structure. The moral Confucian and the instinctively moral Taoist are not at odds. But Confucianism served China as an ethic of engagement, while Taoism and Buddhism provided a private and personal way of life. Taoism was a refuge, and a path for self-enlightenment though in its esoteric forms a potentially dangerous side-track.

It was the image of the Confucian gentleman, benevolent, honest, courteous, and reticent that inspired Chinese public service. 'Observe what he does,' said Confucius, 'enquire into his motives, find out what gives him peace. Can a man hide himself? Can a man hide?' and he was alert to the difficulties. 'The wise person knows about what is right, the inferior person knows only about what will pay.'

It was a tough ethic to adhere to, a standard of behaviour that asked for seriousness and deference, for generosity and justice, faithfulness to friends and assistance to the young. A virtuous person is reluctant to speak without careful thought. 'When it is difficult to do, how can we be anything other than reluctant to talk about it.' Confucius was realistic about the problems. 'I have still not found anyone who loves virtue as much as beauty'. 'Without rapid speech or good looks it is hard to get anywhere in this generation.'

His instincts were for the solid and straightforward. 'Those with strong spirits and resolute characters, honest in manner, and slow to speak out, they are closest to integrity.' The vision was of a warm and generous society, educated and self-educated, mutually supportive, non-competitive, founded on calm, peace-loving behaviour, and inner virtue. That community of wise people was what Confucius dreamed of. 'It is surely a pleasure to learn and to keep learning constantly? It is surely delightful to have like-minded friends come from distant places? The true philosophers have no resentment even when they live the unrecognised life.'

Confucianism did become obsessed with ritual, even with worship in temples erected to Confucius himself. Rejected by some schools of Confucianism, and mocked by many of the Taoists for its excessive subservience, ridiculous correctness, slavish adherence to etiquette, and wasteful procedures, the concept of *li*, proper and ritualistic behaviour, has formed a central feature of Chinese life. Confucianism had varying degrees of success as an influence on society. It was used as a basis for the examination system in the Western Han dynasty, and in the early T'ang, though its fortunes waned with the increasing influence of Buddhism and Taoism. It was the Sung and later dynasties whose neo-Confucianism made it such a dominant feature of Chinese society. Nevertheless the educated man was expected to have knowledge of the Confucian Classics even though the Taoist Canon became part of the examination system in 741. Taoism became fashionable in the later part of Hsüan-tsung's reign and the Taoist texts such as the Chuang Tzu were given Classic status alongside the Confucian canonical texts. Candidates of Taoist upbringing could be examined in Taoist rather than Confucian texts. Tu Fu was an example of an educated man who, no doubt, as a young man spent long hours learning the texts and understanding the content. Men like Tu were potentially material for a government carried out with honesty and integrity. Yet he was to add one more to the long list of talented individuals in Imperial China who are regarded as moral examples but who failed to make a major impact on the government of their times.

Traveling to the Southern Sacred Peak, Zhang Ruocheng (1722 – 1770)

TU FU

Tu Fu [p. 193] was born in 712 at Shao-ling near Ch'ang-an. Like Wang Wei and Li Po his early talents were recognised but he nevertheless failed the Civil Service examinations in 735. He was to take them for a second time later in life but was failed along with all the other candidates for reasons outside his control. His first failure has been put down to a lack of aptitude for the more practical economic and political questions, or the possibility that his style and content was too 'advanced' for the examiners. It may simply have been errors in preparation, nervousness, over-confidence, or any of the other ways in which good students fail examinations they are expected to pass. Or that, despite what lovers of his poetry feel, he was simply not able enough.

His true talents were for poetry and language rather than administration. The result was that he spent many years in poverty, and was never more than a minor civil servant. He was distantly related to many of the great families of the Empire but his own family was not wealthy or influential and he does not seem to have attempted to exploit connections in the way that Li Po frequently did. He was not a celebrated poet in the way Li was, nor established like Wang Wei. His meetings with Li Po clearly impressed him deeply and provide an interesting contrast of temperaments. Li Po's yearning for a depth beyond the visible world, his regret at not being able to reach the mystery he dreams about or achieve a compensating tranquillity in his thoughts, pervade his poetry. Tu Fu's life was the Confucian life of practical realities, a life of survival, of family and domestic affairs, of quiet friendship and acceptance of reality.

Tu sees things clearly and coolly. His greatness is the greatness of the humane eye, that compassionate recognition of existence, that resignation to how things are, that makes him a poet of fate, of the workings of the real world, and a clear mirror for the turbulence and painfulness, the bitterness and poignancy of his times. Again it is interesting to contrast Tu with Wang Wei. Wang is the poet of a tranquil and meditative world, where nature provides a correlative of inner harmony and peace. Wang is self-contained, working to transmute and transcend his feelings even when they run most deeply. His aim is to be 'a thousand miles of quiet evening cloud'. The deaths of those close to him affected him greatly, his wife, his mother, his friend Yin Yao. His sadness and melancholy at death, loss and transience are mirrored in nature by the inner silence and neutrality of the physical world, its lack of an inward life, of mind. He turns to the inner Void in order to reconcile himself to the outer. He knows that strange loneliness and hollowness that we can feel looking at a vast distant landscape or at an evening view, suddenly so remote from and alien to the human, uncaring of us and our reality. It is mind as a process lost among things, the body as an object lost amongst processes. It is a cool but beautiful world where the very neutrality offers a solace. This is Nature not inimical to humanity, nor benevolent, merely apart from us.

That stasis, the solace, is not valid for Li Po, who is always in movement, always presenting a dynamic relationship between self and nature, self and others, or between others. Li is the poet of relationship. His solitudes are in tension with the 'world of humankind', they are solitudes because no one else is there, or someone else is not there. The invisible presence makes, by contrast, the present solitude. Li's stillnesses are a contemplation of emotional relationship: his sadnesses are at the failure of relationship due to his own restless temperament, or the nature of reality. His yearnings are like Shelley's, though less desperately, for a magical paradise where his instability might be a stability. There his restlessness might be a mode of being in that place, his senses might be both stimulated and lulled, his mind might be excited and yet his heart calm. He is always pursuing Shelley's 'Spirit of Delight' or regretting its non-appearance, or drowning its absence in wine.

Where Li is the poet of self as a set of emotional relationships, and Wang Wei is the poet of self as the location of the perception of the inner loneliness of nature, Tu Fu is self as it stands within the world. His honesty and compassion have often been noted. But sanity is his keynote, a balanced attitude that is wholly realistic but wholly human. It is the Confucian clarity and bedrock integrity.

The honesty and straightforwardness, the balance and level-headed realism are there in his poem 'For Wei Pa' [p. 206] or in 'A Visitor' [p. 204]. The compassion is there in his 'Ballad of the War Wagons' [p. 199] and 'The

Homecoming' [p. 201] where his instinct for, and loyalty to, family appears as it does in *'Moon at Night in Ch'ang-an'* [p. 197]. He is the poet of mind (*yi*) and deliberate creativity (*tu-tsao*). It made him a master of strict, dense and complex form. In a tradition where the Confucian values were admired Tu Fu is the quintessential Chinese gentleman, nobility of spirit combining with pragmatic morality and imaginative feeling to emphasise his solidity. He is the ancient tree of one of his poems 'with branches of green bronze and granite roots' exposed to the elements, but tough and straight, not able to be easily made use of because of its nature, but admired for its qualities. If, in moments when we are temporarily out of sympathy with them, Wang Wei can seem too self-centred and quietist, and Li Po too irresponsible and sensation-seeking, then Tu Fu can seem cold with the chill of moral rectitude. But the converse is also true, that Tu Fu has a stability Li lacks and a full engagement with his age that Wang sometimes evades.

Reciting Poetry before the Yellowing of Autumn, Wu Li（1632 – 1718）

THE AN LU-SHAN REBELLION

An Lu-shan, frustrated by the state of the Empire, seeing an opportunity for himself, wanting to protect his own position, or from a mixture of these motives, moved his army south from Peking on the eleventh day of the eleventh month of 755. His claimed objective was the removal of the unpopular Chief Minister Yang Kuo-chung, who was building troop concentrations loyal to himself. His purpose was not the overthrow of the Emperor, though this was no doubt part of the cloud of propaganda against him issued at the time. He had considerable forces, amassed on his own initiative and through the Imperial policy of autonomous border troop concentrations. He relied on military power, the element of surprise, and the disorganisation of the Imperial Court. It was a bold throw of the dice.

In a month he had crossed the Yellow River north of Kaifeng and taken the eastern capital Loyang. There was then a pause in hostilities. Early in 756 An Lu-shan proclaimed a new Dynasty and there was sporadic conflict through the spring and early summer. An Lu-shan does not appear to have had a coherent strategy to secure lines of communication or control the major routes.

On the first of July the Emperor's general Li Kuang-pi inflicted a major defeat on the rebel army near Chenting in the north. There was a possibility that An Lu-shan would be forced to withdraw somehow to his base in Peking and regroup. However, an Imperial blunder opened the way to Ch'ang-an. The T'ung Kuan (Tungkwan), the eastern pass protecting the capital, had been held successfully by the Imperial general Ko-shu Han. It is said that Yang Kuo-chung nervous that Ko-shu Han would switch sides, move against him, or even foment a separate rebellion, persuaded the Emperor to order the general to take the offensive against An Lu-shan. Repeated commands forced Ko-shu Han to leave the pass and engage the rebels. His army was destroyed. Out of a quarter of a million men, mainly highlanders of Ch'in, only a few thousand survived the battle. Tu Fu refers to this in his poem *The Homecoming* [p. 201]. Ko-shu Han took a high rank in the rebel régime, so he may have had rebel sympathies, or perhaps was merely being opportunist. He was eventually imprisoned and executed.

Ten days after the defeat at the pass the rebels entered Ch'ang-an. At dawn on the fourteenth of July the Emperor had secretly abandoned the capital. Yang Kuei-fei and her sisters and Yang Kuo-chung left with him, with members of the Imperial family, the group protected by the army. What followed is the subject of Po Chü-Yi's poem 'The Everlasting Sorrow' [p. 215], a story dwelt on endlessly in later Chinese and Japanese culture. Leaving behind a city in panic and confusion the Emperor's army headed for the south-western route to Ch'êng-tu in Szechwan. On the fifteenth they reached Ma-wei, a post station beside the river, forty miles or so to the west of Ch'ang-an. In a confused scene Yang Kuo-chung was attacked and killed by loyal soldiers of the Imperial army, suspicious of his intentions, and no doubt blaming him, and the Yang family's power over the Empire, for the disaster. Yang Kuei-fei, despite the Emperor's pleas, was then, according to one version of the story, taken from the post-station to a pear orchard near a Buddhist monastery where she was strangled. Her body was shown to the army, who proclaimed their loyalty, and the Emperor, grieving, fled towards Szechwan.

Here Yang Kuei-fei's fate turns into legend. Hers was the delicate white jade face, pale as pear blossom, tinged as Sei Shōnagon says in the Pillow Book with pink so faint as to create doubt whether it was there or not. The Emperor's infatuation with her and her unhappy influence on him is paralleled and described in the opening chapter of the Tale of Genji. To the grieving Emperor, filled with hopeless longing, the memory of his lost love, her face and manner, is like 'Reality in the depths of night...insubstantial as a light-filled dream.' He wanders in nightmare, as if cursed from a previous existence. Blasted by such an intensity of passion that he is left alone and desolate he finds nothing in the world outside that can conjure up her image.

Po Chü-Yi's poem tells how a Taoist adept goes on a shamanistic flight to the magical islands of the Immortals in the eastern seas to find her. She gives him tokens to return with, breaking a decorated box and a hairpin in two, giving him half of each. When he asks for a secret known only to the Emperor and herself as a proof that he has seen her, she tells him about a vow they both had made. They were in the summer palace on that night in the year when the stars Altair and Vega, the Herdboy and Weaver-girl, were allowed to meet in the sky (the seventh night of the seventh month).

At midnight the Emperor dismissed his attendants, and much moved they looked up together at the night sky and, in tears, swore to be husband and wife through all future lives. In Genji, it is said that the Emperor and his lady used to repeat Po Chü-Yi's lines 'to fly together in the sky, two birds on the same wing, to grow together on the earth, two branches of one tree.' When the Taoist wizard returns and describes all this, the Chinese Emperor is stunned with grief.

Chang-an, the city of a million people, experienced the arrival of An Lu-shan's Tartar army accompanied by massacre and looting. Wang Wei, unable to follow the fleeing Court, was captured by the rebels, and is supposed to have pretended to be a deaf-mute and to have attempted suicide. Under pressure he was coerced into accepting office under the rebel Government. Later he wrote a poem claiming that he wept when he saw the new Court enjoying outings with artists and musicians on the Imperial lake. Li Po was at Ch'ih-chou on the Yangtze during this time and so outside the scenes of immediate turmoil, while Tu Fu was temporarily absent at the moment when the city fell. But in the autumn Tu Fu was once more in the capital. His poem 'By the Waters of Wei' [p. 198] is set amongst the great houses along the banks of the pleasure lake, emptied, shuttered and abandoned. He draws an analogy between Yang Kuei-fei and her sisters and the Han consort, Flying Swallow, enjoying the flower-filled gardens and sending men to execution with a glance and a cruel smile. Her fate is also the fate of Ch'ang-an, trampled into the dust. The remaining representative of the Tang Empire is Su-tsung the son of the Emperor, Hsüan-tsung having abdicated, who is at Feng-hsiang about 100 miles to the west. He is now 'The Emperor in the North'

Tu Fu was still in the capital in early 757, separated from his family who he had left at Fu-chou in the north. 'Spring in Ch'ang-an' [p. 196] is a poem of resignation to fate, but also one of hope since even in a fallen Empire and an occupied city nature remains inviolable. The ambiguous grammatical construction of the second couplet identifies his tears of separation and painful memory with the dew spilling from the flowers, and his own fears for his family with the secret anxieties of the wild birds caught in the turmoil of the capital. The beacons on the hills are burning month after month signalling the continuing civil war, and news from home is scarce. 'Moon at Night in Ch'ang-an' [p. 197] is another poem of separation and absence, belying any view that Tu Fu lacks the deeper emotions. On the contrary the feelings are the more profound for being directed towards his wife and children. It is in a poem like this, in the steadiness of his gaze, that Tu can make Li Po seem superficial and disengaged, and Wang Wei seem pliable and low-profile.

In the previous autumn of 756, Prince Lin, a son of the emperor had command of a southern army based on Chiang-ling on the Yangtze. Lin began to build forces and supplies out of proportion to his role, and a nervous Su-tsung ordered him to report to the ex-Emperor in his refuge of Ch'êng-tu. Prince Lin ignored the order and his flotilla set off down the Yangtze. Lin apparently intended to set up an alternative government in the Yangtze delta.

Li Po meanwhile had taken refuge in the Lu Shan mountains south-east of Kiukiang on the Yangtze. His wife joined him from Kweiteh (near Kaifeng), in the north, after a long separation. She was accompanied by her brother, to whom Li confessed himself a less than an ideal brother-in-law. He said that he was ashamed to be waited on by his distinguished sister. At Kiukiang his wife visited Li Lin-fu's daughter who was living as a Taoist nun on the Lu Shan. Li writes *a poem* [p. 186] to her there in 'that refuge'. 'You follow the Tao, seek out Immortals, catch the blue clouds in your white hands, trail your skirt of gauze through purple mists.' There the disaster of their society is more endurable. 'The blue mountains are themselves blue mountains,' says the Zenrin, of the natural world that is contained within itself, outside any human contrivance, 'The white clouds are themselves white clouds.'

When Prince Lin reached Kiukiang in early 757, and the port was 'a mass of military banners', Li Po innocently joined the expedition. He probably believed it to be part of the Imperial opposition to An Lu-shan who was in fact murdered by his son about this time. The son An Ch'ing-hsü then became the Rebel leader. Prince Lin had already been disowned by the Emperor. Joining the expedition gave Li an opportunity to mix with Court circles again, to enjoy the banquets and the dancing girls, the wine and the music, as the flotilla sailed down the Yangtze River, and to celebrate it in extravagant verse, his Songs of the Progress to the East. Near Yangchow however the fleet encountered Government forces, Prince

Lin's Generals abandoned him. He was defeated in a river-battle and escaped to the south. He was subsequently captured and executed.

Li Po had fled from Yangchow, but was arrested as he returned to Kiukiang, and imprisoned, despite his protestations that he had been deceived, had joined the expedition to fight the rebels, and had broken with Prince Lin as soon as he had realised what was happening. His wife was at Yü-chang seventy miles south and attempted to intercede for him. He wrote to the new Chief Minister Ts'ui Huan asking for forgiveness, and was freed in the autumn by a passing official Sung Jo-ssu after a review of his case. Within a few weeks the Imperial forces had liberated Ch'ang-an and Lo-yang.

The fifty-eight year old Wang Wei was working for the Rebel Government in Ch'ang-an when it was recaptured. He escaped execution but was charged with collaboration and imprisoned in the Bodhi Temple. There he composes and recites two poems to his friend Pei Ti. The first portrays the confusion and desolation as the city is taken over by the Rebels, who 'make music on the green waters of the lake'. The second 'Words spoken to Pei Ti' [p. 157] expresses the desire to escape from enforced Rebel service. The poems and the intercession of his brother and others gained his release. He returned to the Government and was later in service as an official of the Council of State (until his death in 761).

Tu Fu meanwhile had joined the new Emperor at his temporary capital of Feng-hsiang a hundred miles west of Ch'ang-an. Since ordinary methods of recruitment for official service had ceased to operate because of the Rebellion he was able to enter without examination. So at the age of forty-five he at last held a modest position close to the Court. It lasted only a few months. He seems to have been over-zealous, or too courageous in going against the Emperor's wishes. Whatever the reason in the October of 757 he left Feng-hsiang on leave, to journey to meet his wife and family whom he had not seen since the previous year. 'The Homecoming' [p. 201] describes the trek of some two hundred miles across the hills northwest of Ch'ang-an. He travelled from Feng-hsiang northeast to Pin-chou on the Ching River, and then northeast again to Fu-chou on the Luo river due north of of Chang-an. His family in Fu-chou consisted of his two daughters and two sons, one still a baby born during his 'detention' in Ch'ang-an.

Later in 759 we find that Tu who had not returned to the Court was a local Commissioner of Education and against the background of a country still in turmoil was sent to Loyang by the prefect of the District. He stayed on the way with a friend, recalled in 'For Wei Pa' [p. 206], who was an unemployed minor official. Later in that year again he gave up the post, which he disliked, and moved with his family to Ch'êng-tu in the Red Basin of Szechwan.

Li Po was taken into Sung Jo-ssu's service but in 758 had left again and was lying ill near Lukiang in Anhui. The Chief Minister Ts'ui Huan who had approved his release from prison fell from power. Li Po's sentence was reversed and he was now banished to Yeh-lang in the upper reaches of the Yangtze, in Yünnan in the far southwest. He started on a long, and deliberately slow, journey along the Yangtze, staying first with officials who were old friends near Hankow, at Wu-ch'ang and Han-yang. There he drank with old friends and watched 'the girls in their gauze dresses, dancing to the high notes of flutes, their songs climbing to the clouds.' He was still trying to work his contacts at Court but despite an amnesty for others was again travelling upriver in the spring of 759.

The poem 'Remembering the Springs at Ch'ih-chou' [p. 191] already anticipates his return from exile, and shortly after reaching the Yangtze Gorges in the third month of 759 he was pardoned in a general amnesty which recalled those in exile. By early autumn he had sailed downriver again and was at Yo-chou near the Tung-t'ing Lake.

China was still in turmoil with fresh revolts and rebellions; An Lu-shan's son was assassinated and replaced; there were new Government defeats; and Lo-yang fell to a second rebel army. In the ninth month Yo-chou was under threat from a new southern uprising, as the rebellion fragmented into local rebellions and revolts, and it was the end of the year before Li could escape downriver to Wu-ch'ang. From there he drifted back to the Nanking area, where, dogged by illness, he spent his last few years, still attempting to gain official employment. At the end of 762 the sixty-one year old Li was lying desperately ill at the home of the famous calligrapher

Li Yang-ping, the Prefect of Tang-t'u (Taiping) on the Yangtze near Nanking. Li Po gave him the separate sheets of hundreds of his poems before his death. Unlike the more fortunate Wang Wei, Li Po died while still in what he must have seen as an equivalent of exile, far from Ch'ang-an, having missed all his life the high office he had believed he merited.

Tu Fu the younger poet still remained in Ch'êng-tu. He owned a small cottage, and carried out literary work for local patrons. Living among the network of rivers and streams that descend from the mountains to flow around Ch'eng-tu, in ill-health and probably consumptive, he wrote some of the quietest and most resigned lyrics of his last and greatest poetic period. 'A Visitor' is set amongst the spring waters, striking a note of realism and a gentle self-deprecating awareness. His poem 'For General Hua' is again set among the waters and high skies, the clouds and remoteness of Ch'êng-tu. It was a gentle Confucian warning to the headstrong young General that it was wise to keep to the Middle Way, not to be tempted by ambition to covet illicit power, behave immorally, or aim at the Imperial role reserved for the Son of Heaven.

In 765 Tu's chief patron died. He had held a nominal official appointment as a Consultant Assistant-Secretary at the Ministry of Works, advising the Provincial Governor, and receiving a small salary. He was now unemployed and he left Ch'eng-tu travelling down the Yangtze, reaching K'uei-chou, White King city, upstream from the Wu and Ch'ü-t'ang gorges, in 766. During his two years there he wrote many of his greatest poems. 'Yangtze' [p. 210] invokes an autumnal mood and the transience of life, contrasting the turbid human river of existence and the eternal clear star-river of the Galaxy. He is living his twilight in the broken Empire, his thoughts now for a moment clear. The human past has been destroyed, but the Courts of the Heavens are still in place, the Moon's circle still perfect, ever renewed. His own sick body is itself a dew-drenched clock that counts the final hours, and it is bowed down by his inner sadness, as the flowers are weighed down by chill night dew.

In 'High and Dry on the Yangtze' [p. 209] in the gibbon-haunted gorges near K'uei-chou he looks back through the same cool autumn light, with the same clarity of vision, on his real and his metaphorical journey. The mind, that mind which creates the poem and in a limited and impersonal way lives on within language, looks with irony and pity on the body that is so ill it can no longer even escape itself through wine.

In 'Night Journey Thoughts'[p. 195], Tu is on the Yangtze on his voyage in 768-9 down river across the Tung-t'ing Lake and up the Hsiang River by Ch'ang-sha. In his objective, solitary, and starlit vision he is the lone white gull floating on the random currents of the air. 'Deep Winter'[p. 211] written in the same region is almost an extended metaphor for his situation. He is the last survivor of the three great poets. Tu Fu the clear-eyed. In a last gentle poem 'Meeting Li Kuei-Nien'[p. 212] four lines are enough to remember the past greatness, celebrate friendship and creativity, and appreciate a moment of peace and the spring warmth of the south, even though it is a last place, where the petals fall, along with poems, years, lives and empires.

Old Trees by a Cold Waterfall, Wen Zhengming (1470 - 1559)

THE T'ANG DYNASTY AND TIME

The T'ang Dynasty reveals its consciousness of, and preoccupation with, time. The Tao that is eternal and invisible energy manifests itself in temporal things, in visible process. The T'ang Dynasty sees itself in a long continuum of Chinese history. 'Hold fast to the oldest Way', says the Tao Te Ching, 'to understand the Present Time. To know the root of the Past is the thread that runs through the Way.' T'ang looks back to Han, to the past lives of great individuals whose memory it cherishes.

The Emperor fulfils a role beyond man, as a mediator between the eternal and the ephemeral. His vows may carry through many existences, since Buddhism claims that the spirit is bound on the Wheel of Lives unless it can achieve release in Nirvana. Equally there may be only one life, so that he must strive also to become a Taoist Immortal. T'ang poems remember Emperor Wu of Han, who, obsessed by the desire for everlasting life, set up dew-pans held by bronze immortals to catch the elixir of Heaven. Buried at Mao-ling, Leafy Mound, he is remembered as 'Young Liu in Leafy Mound' whose life and dynasty vanished swifter than the wind.

Immortality is always out of reach. The Wheel of Lives is always turning. The living Emperor is caught between everlastingness and nothingness, between the desire for and the escape from immortality. Through the poems as through the palaces there is the sound of dripping water clocks, of bells and drums tolling the hours. Moon, sun and stars move over Heavens where time congeals in dew, is mirrored in water, is reflected from bronze.

Life though is transient, love and empires grow cold, or are destroyed, the blossom is forever falling from the trees, autumn ruins the leaves, courtyards fill with weeds, beauty grows old with neglect and inattention. Yet everything stirs with the vortex, birds are always in flight, the silk curtains blow, there is a cool wind in the pines, wine and songs flow like the waters, hearts are high as clouds that drift over the mountains. Li Po *dances with his shadow* [p. 170]. Tu Fu watches *the bent grasses in a river-breeze* [p. 195]. Wang Wei is *blown like thistle-seed* [p. 156] across the northern wastes of the Empire. Rain falls, rivers flow, cloud moves, light alters.

Wang Wei knows a way to defeat time if he could only follow it. Through meditation on the Void we enter the timeless, the Moment, the Now, where there are no names or forms, where language is still and only being exists. It is the place Nature inhabits, free of mind. Or it is the place where everything within the self has become mind and therefore mindless. It is Nature, without thought, without memory, without intention. It is Nature, without ownership, without demands, without authority.

And he knows another way, a way of creation, where the painting freezes time in order to re-create itself in the eye of the observer, in the eye's living time. The way of the poem also, where time runs within a closed form, within a frame of words and characters, and is an object as a painting is. The painting and the poem are landscapes that wait for an eye to make them live again. They persist in time, wait and wake in time, contain a time, a moment of time, and spill over into other times. Art escapes life to capture life, denies the creator immortality in the body while achieving its own immortality of form, and carrying a meaning and purpose to come. Wang Wei, destroyed again and again by loss, by the death of others, cannot reach the silence he yearns for, can only recreate the Now in ink, on silk, in the mind, again and again, as artist, in intensity.

Li Po is possessed by transience: Li the restless who is the wanderer and the searcher after immortality. He traverses China from Szechwan to Shantung, from Peking to the Yangtze Delta: Li who can compose in a flash, in a lightning stroke. Who drinks to lose time, to make time vanish, to escape reality in stupor, and consciousness in sleep: Li who can almost touch and feel the tranquillity and stillness of others, but rarely his own. Li who is so far below the hills, that the adepts seem to climb, who is dizzied by height, who has to descend the mountains, and abandon the hills: Li who is *'knee-deep in a thousand fallen flowers'* [p. 172]: Li whose emblems are the Moon and the mirror. Li who dreams he is the butterfly, who is 'helpless' in the deep garden. Li who is the transience of colours, and the beauty of sunsets, lost notes of music, lost poems fluttering, lost hours, girls, wine-cups, lost emotions: Li whose inner movement is the spirit journey, the *hsien*'s flight through the night, through the Heavens: Li, who is the shaman from the East, the lone magician of Asia, who can ride through the air, unaided. Li who can visit the timeless Paradises of the West, the Magic Islands of the East, and return, as Keats's knight returns, to a world of time that is inadequate to his senses and his aspirations. Li who longs for the alchemy that will transcend time, that will *'transmute his bones to gold'* [p. 191], to that fused silver moon and golden sun of the Taoist Eternal Child. Li who like Baudelaire in 'The Voyage' is always ready to set sail one more time, to move on, into the unknown, to find the new.

Tu Fu is the eye that sees the Moment. He is the self-awareness of the intellect, the perception of form and its intricacies, the observer of time as History being made, History as it defines the human and the inhuman, as it enters into memory, as it remains in the present through its creations and its transformations. Tu is the lone element of being, wandering on the surface of the real, driven by the wind, or caught in the walls of the whirlpool. He is the observer of the neutrality of the universe, and the neutrality of the vortex of historical events, of the twin sets of forces that emerge from them to touch the individual. He is the inhabitant of a universe which is neither benevolent as his Confucianism taught, nor in any way malevolent.

The universe is not indifferent, hostile, alien, or malign, since these are all words that imply sentience, feeling or attitude. It is insensible, without mind, an ocean of energies. Tu is the eye behind the crystal blind, the eye that gazes and is filled with sympathy, energy, delight or tears. He sees those things that are embedded in time, arts and ethics, laws and rituals. He is a Confucian in his humanity, his humility, his warmth, his power to endure and to create within the world. He knows the pain of fitting human nature to a social order, and the pain of seeing order descend into human chaos. He counters pain with feeling, sensibility, creativity, strength of mind, compassion and good will. He knows the human world is subject to time, and therefore to loss, regret, irretrievable error. He knows that turmoil of politics where as the old song of Ch'u says 'loyalty brings disaster'. He also sees within the strands of event, natural beauty and natural affection, transient but deep, ephemeral but consoling. In the natural, in his personal Taoist depths, Tu Fu is calm, simple, tranquil.

The Tao is the matrix of time, and it creates the forms of time. Attempting to understand what lies behind 'the how' of the universe Chuang-tzu says, 'Things appear to us, but we do not understand where they come from. They emerge into the world, but no one sees the portal.

We value what is known, but do not know how to use the unknown.' In western terms we produce a scientific description of how events succeed each other, what changes we expect to see, and the appearance of the 'surfaces' of our experience. But we delude ourselves if we believe that we grasp the 'inner nature' of energy, or change, of 'being here' and 'changing into'.

The whole thrust of critical sceptical philosophy, of epistemology, in the West, since Hume and Kant, has been to mark out empirically, through observation and meditation the limits of human understanding in thought and language. The Tao is not deity. It does not produce by intentional design. It is unknown and unknowing. The vortex of its events produces space and time. It is the waves, the oscillations, the regular vibrations we use to measure the succession of events we call time. And it is the contiguities that we use to measure immediate space, and therefore the speed of light and by deduction the distances of the remote universe.

The Tao exists in itself and not for itself. Taoism attempts to loosen the bonds that bind us, to free us from time. Its aspiration is not to understand nature, but to *be* nature. 'The wise put Self last and it comes first' says the Tao Te Ching. Its method is to work 'without action', *wu-wei*, that is without self-conscious intent, without striving or stress, without endless words. Its tenor is calmness, to be the water surface that reflects light without intention, that accepts images without grasping, and retains them without possessing. Its appearance is an uncultivated innocence 'sorrowful like a baby that has lost its mother, stupid like one who has lost the way' as Chuang-tzu says, tongue in cheek. If the natural world cannot be trusted in its lack of intent, what can? If simplicity will not get us there, how will complexity achieve it?

Being never quite at ease, that is the dangerous road for the mind. To be, on the other hand, a creative source, to make the difficult happen as if spontaneously, to concentrate the mind on the object until the self vanishes, without being aware that it has vanished, is the Way. In this our greatest enemy is our sense of time. We find beauty in the timeless, virtue in the selfless, truth in the un-carved and unadorned. Though we, through natural selection, are nothing if not the creatures of time, the result of event, the products of the sieve of generations, the stability that preserves mutation, we are also that which contemplates time, reflects on process, inhabits the Now. Not to be lost in language games is the Way, not to believe, not to follow, not to own. Death does not exist for the self, only dying. Dying is the vanishing of self-consciousness. To be aware and conscious, but without self-consciousness, is to have vanished as a smile vanishes or a thought.

Liberation from time is achieved by destroying the grasping, the desire that links us to time. 'How can I free myself?' asks the pupil. 'Who is imprisoning you?' says the Master. 'No one' replies the pupil. 'Then why do you seek to be free?' Not to contemplate, or to concentrate, to strain at awareness, or to restrain the body, but to eliminate thought is the Way: to abandon learning and embrace the natural.

In it there is nothing special. There is no mystical concept to be grasped, no higher essence to be striven for. It is difficult because it is so simple, so contrary to the idea of 'progress' and 'culture', to the ways of power or science, 'truth' or religion, self-conscious morality or social planning. The world is simply there. We are simply beings. What we strive after in time is only achievable through the timeless. What we yearn for is already there, unchanged by our yearning. 'Mount Lu in mist and rain, the River Che in flood. Before I saw them, to see them - endless longing. I went there and came back. There was nothing special. Mount Lu in mist and rain, the River Che in flood.'

Time is not the sky and the river. Time is the mind conscious of change. To escape from time is not to 'enter' a realm called the timeless, or to 'fall' into the Void. There is nowhere to fall to out of this world. There is no place to be in that is not in time, because both world and time are in this mind. Then why is living so difficult for us?

Time in the mind is memory. Memory feeds regret and anticipation, hope and disillusionment. We store mind in objects and in language, in mathematics and in scientific theory, in buildings and in events, in the processes and the things we create, even in our affections, even in our love. The object, the words, the notation, the history, the love, may be preserved even when the transient human body dies, and in turn they may create thought and feeling in a living mind. Everything we make and do tells what we are. 'Where can a man hide? Where can a man hide?' Memory is mind's magic and its fate. Memory is mind's hurt and its delight. Our whole past lives that are present in the living 'Now', are nothing but memory. The poetry and the history of the T'ang Dynasty are still here. The pictures are in the poems, even though the T'ang Dynasty itself is gone, like water or clouds.

T'AO CH'IEN (365-427 AD)

Scholars in a Landscape, 16th century

T'ao Ch'ien (365-427 AD)

RETURNING TO LIVE IN THE COUNTRY

Young, I was always free of common feeling.
It was in my nature to love the hills and mountains.
Mindlessly I was caught in the dust-filled trap.
 Waking up, thirty years had gone.
The caged bird wants the old trees and air.
Fish in their pool miss the ancient stream.
I plough the earth at the edge of South Moor.
Keeping life simple, return to my plot and garden.
My place is hardly more than a few fields.
 My house has eight or nine small rooms.
Elm-trees and Willows shade the back.
Plum-trees and Peach-trees reach the door.
Misted, misted the distant village.
Drifting, the soft swirls of smoke.
Somewhere a dog barks deep in the winding lanes.
A cockerel crows from the top of the mulberry tree.
No heat and dust behind my closed doors.
My bare rooms are filled with space and silence.
Too long a prisoner, captive in a cage,
Now I can get back again to Nature.

RETURNING TO LIVE IN THE COUNTRY II

I always loved to walk the woods and mountains.
Pleased myself, lost in fields and marshes.
Now I go out with nephews, nieces,
In the wilds, parting hazel branches,
Back and forth through the mounds and hollows,
All around us signs of ancient peoples,
Remnants of their broken hearths and well-heads,
Mulberry and bamboo groves neglected.
Stop and ask the simple woodsman,
'Where have all these people gone now?'
Turning he looks quietly and tells me,
'Nothing's left of them, they're finished.'
One world. Though the lives we lead are different,
In courts of power or labouring in the market,
These I know are more than empty words:
Our life's a play of light and shade,
Returning at last to the Void.

READING THE CLASSIC OF HILLS AND SEAS

In the summer grass and trees have grown.

Over my roof the branches meet.

Birds settle in the leaves.

I enjoy my humble place.

Ploughing's done, the ground is sown,

Time to sit and read my book.

The narrow deeply-rutted lane

Means my friends forget to call.

Content, I pour the new Spring wine,

Go out and gather food I've grown.

A light rain from the East,

Blows in on a pleasant breeze.

I read the story of King Mu,

See pictures of the Hills and Seas.

One glance finds all of heaven and earth.

What pleasures can compare with these?

Note: King Mu (1001-947BC) of the Chou Dynasty dined with the Queen of the Immortals, Si Wang Mu, in the Western Paradise (among the Kun-lun mountains of Tibet). There she tended the garden where the peach-tree grew that supported the Universe. Her Paradise was that of exalted purity, the jade or pearl mountain, entered through a golden door. The peaches conferred immortality. She later visited Emperor Wu Ti of Han (r.141-97BC) riding on a white dragon, gave him a peach from the tree, and taught him the secrets of eternal life. Wu built a tower with a golden vase on its summit to collect the pure dew that dripped from the stars.

DRINKING THE WINE

I built my house near where others live.
Still there's no sound of wheels or voices.
You'll ask me 'How can that be?'
When the mind is remote the place is distant.
Cutting Chrysanthemums by the Eastern Hedge,
I look out towards the Southern Hills.
Mountain air is fine at end of day.
The flights of birds make for home.
In these things there is a hint of Truth,
but trying to tell it there's no mind, no words.

T'ao Ch'ien (365-427 AD)

Ninth Day, Ninth Month

Slowly autumn comes to an end.
Painfully cold a dawn wind thicks the dew.
Grass round here will not be green again,
Trees and leaves are already suffering.
The clear air is drained and purified
And the high white sky's a mystery.
Nothing's left of the cicada's sound.
Flying geese break the heavens' silence.
The Myriad Creatures rise and return.
How can life and death not be hard?
From the beginning all things have to die.
Thinking of it can bruise the heart.
What can I do to lighten my thoughts?
Solace myself drinking the last of this wine.
Who understands the next thousand years?
Let's just make this morning last forever.

PEACH BLOSSOM SPRING

(an adaptation of T'ao Ch'ien's Story)

A fisherman journeying along a stream reached a place where the banks were filled with Peach Blossom. There were fallen petals everywhere and a deep fragrance. The peach groves ended at the source of the stream where a spring came out of the hillside. There he saw a narrow opening out of which light shone. He left his boat and went inside. He reached a land where everyone seemed happy. The people all came to see him and question him. They said their ancestors had travelled there to escape from the empire of Ch'in and that no one had ever wished to return. They knew nothing of the dynasties of Han and Wei and were amazed at what he told them. He stayed for a while and before leaving they told him that nothing would be gained by revealing their existence to anyone else.

When he emerged from the hill he took to his boat and retraced his journey noting every turning. When he returned home he told about his adventure. He was sent back with others to show them the route but it was lost. And no one ever found their way there again.

⤜ WANG WEI (699-759 AD) ⤛

An Autumn Scene with Birds, Xu Daoning (10th–13th century)

LETTER TO P'EI TI

This month the weather has been bright and clear, and I could have crossed the mountains. But I was reluctant to trouble you, knowing you were deep in the Classics. So I wandered around the mountain, stayed at Kan-p'ei Temple, ate with the monks, and wandered home again. Then I went north over the Yüan-pa, under a clear moon. At night I climbed Hua-tzu Hill, and watched the moonlight on the Yang River's ripples. Far-off, lights on the cold mountain glittered then vanished. A dog in the deep lanes barked like a leopard. The pounding of grain in the night sounded between strokes of a distant bell. Now I am sitting alone listening to the silence. I think a lot about the old days, when we made poems together, climbing the steep tracks by clear streams. We must wait till the trees and grass grow green again, and, idling in spring hills, we can see fish leap in the light, the gulls soar, the white dew on green moss. At dawn we will hear the birds call in the fields. It is not long till then, when you could come wandering with me. If I did not know your natural sensibility, I would hold back from making even this indirect invitation. I speak from a deep impulse, but it is not pressing.

From Wang Wei, the mountain man

GREEN-WATER STREAM

To reach the Yellow-Flowered River
Go by the Green-Water Stream.
A thousand twists and turns of mountain
But the way there can't be many miles.
The sound of water falling over rocks
And deep colour among pines.
Gently green floating water-plants.
Bright the mirrored reeds and rushes.
I am a lover of true quietness.
Watching the flow of clear water
I dream of sitting on the uncarved rock
casting a line on the endless stream.

Note: The uncarved rock is the Tao.
       The endless stream is the Tao.

Wang Wei (699-759 AD)

IN ANSWER

In these quiet years growing calmer,
Lacking knowledge of the world's affairs,
I stop worrying how things will turn out.
My quiet mind makes no subtle plans.
Returning to the woods I love
A pine-tree breeze rustles in my robes.
Mountain moonlight fills the lute's bowl,
Shows up what learning I have left.
If you ask what makes us rich or poor
Hear the Fisherman's voice float to shore.

Note: In the old tale the message of the Fisherman is that the Taoist must dip his feet in the muddy water (of the world) but should wash his hat-strings in the clear water (of the Tao).

PEACH BLOSSOM SPRING

A fisherman floated on, enjoying Spring.
The shores, he found, were covered in Peach Blossom.
Watched reddening trees, uncertain where he was.
Seeing no one reached green water springs.
There a way led through the hill.
Twisting, turning to a vast plain.
Distant trees rose to the clouds.
Houses stretched among bamboo and flowers.
Woodmen had names from times of Chou,
Clothes they wore were those of Ch'in,
Once had lived near Wu-ling River,
Now they lived outside the world.
Bright moon in pines. By their doors peace.
Sunrise. From clouds the wild birds call.
Amazed, they want to see this stranger,
Invite him; ask questions of his country.
At first light they sweep flowers from the gate.
At dusk fishermen, woodmen ride the stream.
They had sought refuge there from the world,
Became Immortals, never returned.

Who in those hills can know the world of men,
Who, gazing out, sees only clouds and hills?
He forgot Paradise is hard to find.
His spirit turned again to his own home.
Leaving those hidden streams and mountains,
Thought he could return when he wished,

Knew the way. How could he go wrong?

Who can know how hills and valleys alter?

He only knew the deep ways he wandered.

How many green streams in those cloudy woods?

When Spring comes a myriad Peach-filled rivers,

Who knows which one might lead to Paradise?

FOR MÊNG HAO-JAN

Never to see that true friend again.
Han River gleams wide to the east.
I might ask where his island's found.
River and hills. Empty is his place.

Note: Mêng was friend also to Li Po. See the note to Li's tribute.

A REPLY

I have a place on the Chungnan slopes.

Sitting there you can see the Mountains.

No one there, no guests, the gate is closed.

No plans all day, just time and silence.

Nothing stops you gazing and dreaming.

Why not come and try to find me there?

Note: Wang Wei's estate was at Lant'ien, in the Chungnan (South Mountain) foothills about thirty miles south east of the capital Ch'ang-an, and on the Wang River. This was a favourite location for country retreats.

POEM OF FAREWELL

Morning rain on Wei's city
Falls in the soft dust.
Green. The courtyard willows.
Green leaves. The newest.
But you must drink deeper.
Again, one more cup?
Out west where you go
What friendship there?

Wang Wei (699-759 AD)

Mourning Yin Yao

We follow you home to the Mountain.
Back again through oak and green pine.
Beyond the White Clouds you stay forever.
Only this stream runs down to Humankind.

WORDS FOR THE MICA SCREEN

Unfold this screen
Against the light,
Show hills and streams
Nature painted.

CHUNGNAN

Middle-aged now, following the Way.

Settled at evening near the Chungnan slopes.

Delight, and I wander off by myself

Searching for what I need to see alone.

I climb up to the roots of the streams,

Sit and watch the White Clouds pass,

Meet the old man of the woods,

Talk and laugh, forget to go home.

PA PASS

At daybreak I head for Pa Pass.
Spring and I together leave Ch'ang-an.
A woman washes clothes in bright water.
The birds at dawn sing in the light.
River country. Boats here are markets.
Mountain bridges cling to treetops.
Climbing up, a hundred villages.
In the far sun the Two Rivers.
People here speak another language,
But the birdsong's just like my country's.
Understanding the depths of landscape,
Even here I am never lonely.

VISITING THE TEMPLE

Not knowing where the temple was,

I travelled miles on hills of cloud,

Through ancient pines, no good tracks,

Towards bell sounds across deep gorges.

Stream's noise where rocks are high.

Cool sun in fir branches.

Sit at night by the mountain pool,

Seeking to reign in the Dragon.

GOING TO THE TEMPLE

THE TEN STAGES OF PERCEPTION

Up through bamboo. Leave the First Stage:
Pass Illusion: Go by Lotus Mountain:
Through the Pass, there's the whole of Ch'u:
Beyond the woods see the distant plain:
Cross-legged on a mat of grass:
Hear scriptures in the high pine:
Reach the Void: through Clouds of Law:
Meditate to achieve Nirvana.

MEDITATION

Thin cloud. Light rain.
Far cell. Closed to noon.
Sit. Look. Green moss
Becomes one with your clothes.

THE RECLUSE

Every way the emerald trees' shadows.
Each day's green moss free of dust.
Wild-haired, stretch-legged, he sits
By the high pine with half-open eyes.

Wang Wei (699-759 AD)

FROM THE MOUNTAIN

Here there are others like me
Sitting alone in meditation.
Look out here from the city.
All you will see is White Clouds.

NIGHT HILLS

Rain gone. Hills are void.

Night air. Autumn now.

Bright moon in the pines.

Clear stream on the stones.

A bamboo noise – who heads home?

The lotus stirs – who sets out?

Spring scents always go.

But you – you must always stay.

LIVING BY THE RIVER

Back again to this place of refuge.

No more entering the city.

Lean against a tree by the door,

Watch the distant villages below.

Green stems shining in the water,

White birds flying in the hills,

Thinking how that Man from Yüling

Gave up the world to refresh the garden.

LEAVING WANG RIVER

Finally decide to depart,

Sadly let go of ancient pines.

Who can see the last of Blue Hills?

Or bear to leave the Green-Water Stream?

Wang Wei (699-759 AD)

PASSING THE TEMPLE

Tonight he walks with his light stick,
Stops by the Tiger Stream's source,
Asks us to listen to the mountain sound,
Goes home again by clear waters.
Endless blossoms in the stillness.
Bird-cries deep in the valleys.
Now he'll sit in empty hills.
In pine-winds, feel the touch of autumn.

HILL ROAD

Ching River's rocks show white.
Cold air. The sparse red leaves.
Clear of rain these sky-tracks,
Clothes soaked in the blue.

Note: Su Tung-p'o in the eleventh century commenting on a variant of Wang Wei's poem said 'Read his poems closely and there are paintings in the words. Look at his paintings closely and there are poems in the paintings.'

Wang Wei (699-759 AD)

DRIFTING

September skies are clear to the distance.
Clearer still so far from human kind.
A heron by the pool, a mountain cloud,
Either of them makes the mind content.
The faintest ripples still and evening's here.
  The moon turns silver and I dream,
Tonight leaning on a single oar,
Drifting without thought of going home.

LIVING IN THE HILLS

Alone, at peace, I close the door.
Shut out the sky's evening flame.
Cranes settle in the pines.
No one comes to try my gate.
Bamboo tender with new growth.
Red lotus shedding its old sleeves.
A light glows down by the ford.
Gathering water-chestnuts. They come home.

THE STONE LEDGE

On the stone ledge above the water,
Where willow leaf-tips drink the wine.
If you say the spring breeze has no meaning,
Why does it bring me all these falling flowers?

THREE SONGS FOR LADY PAN

Fireflies flash on mica screens.
No echo in Golden Halls.
Seen through gauze the autumn night
Where the lonely light shines.

Autumn grass on Palace yards.
The Emperor no longer cares to see.
How much pain in clear music.
They go past. The Golden Ones.

Court-ladies' blinds are closed.
Courtyards empty. All are gone.
Now they are part of spring gardens,
Flowered voices in the sun.

Note: Pan Chieh-yü was concubine to Emperor Ch'êng of Han but was
slandered and fell from favour. Her own poem of injury reads:

White silk new sliced
Pure as fallen snow,
Cut for a round fan
Bright as the full moon,
Goes always by his side,
Like the tender wind.
But when autumn comes
When cold chills fire,
It will be cast aside.
Love's flame will end.

HOW FINE

I sweep the dust from ancient lines and read.
Wait for the moon. Take strings and play.
By Peach Blossom Spring no word of Han,
By Pines whose titles date from Ch'in.

The valley's empty. Who comes home?
Blue evening hills grow cold.
How fine your refuge is,
Looking out to those White Clouds.

Note: The first Ch'in Emperor a thousand years earlier is said to have given titles to the pines which gave him shelter. Buddhism is also called the thousand-year-old pine.

MISSION

Alone on the road to the border,
Beyond the soil won from the Hun.
I'm blown like thistle-seed out of Han.
Wild geese fly off to barren lands.
Out of the Gobi a puff of smoke.
In the long river a swollen sun.
Our patrol is on the High Pass.
Our camp is on Mount Yenjan.

WORDS SPOKEN TO P'EI TI

How can we break out of the net,
Be free of all this sound and dust,
Swinging a thorn-branch, find the way
Back to Peach Blossom Spring?

Note: Charged with collaboration with the Rebels in occupied Ch'ang-an
this is one of two poems said to have saved Wang's life. Unable to write it
down he recited it, during his internment, to his friend P'ei Ti.

FOR P'EI TI

We've not seen each other
for a long time now.
Each day above the stream
I see us arm in arm.
Memory. Painful goodbyes.
If it feels like this now,
What did it feel like then?

FROM THE WANG RIVER SCROLL

THE BAMBOO GROVE

Sitting alone among dark bamboo,
Play: lift my voice, into deep trees.
Where am I? No one knows.
Only White Moon finds me here.

THE DEER ENCLOSURE

Meet no one on the empty mountain.
Hear only echoes of men's voices.
Light falls through the deep wood,
Shines softly on the green moss.

WRITTEN ON THE WANG RIVER SCROLL

No urge now to write poems.

Old age is my companion.

In error they made me a poet in a past life.

Some lost existence had me as a painter.

Unable to get rid of ingrained habits,

The world has come to know me by them.

My name, my style, they may grasp, it's true.

But my mind and heart they'll never know.

Note: Wang Wei was poet and painter. On the scroll he depicted twenty favourite places, in and around his estate, in scenes and words.

WHITE HAIRS

Once a tiny child now an old man.
White hairs to match the soft down.
How the heart gets hurt by life.
Beyond the Gateless Gate's
Where craving ends.

LI PO (699-762 AD)

Mountain Landscape, Li Di (early 15th century)

GREEN MOUNTAIN

You ask me why I live on Green Mountain –
I smile in silence and the quiet mind.
Peach petals blow on mountain streams
To earths and skies beyond Humankind.

WINE

Drinking, I sit,
Lost to Night,
Keep falling petals
From the ground:
Get up to follow
The stream's white moon,
No sign of birds,
The humans gone.

LINES FOR A TAOIST ADEPT

My friend lives high on East Mountain.

His nature is to love the hills and gorges.

In green spring he sleeps in empty woodland,

Still there when the noon sun brightens.

Pine-tree winds to dust his hair.

Rock-filled streams to cleanse his senses.

Free of all sound and stress,

Resting on a wedge of cloud and mist.

MÊNG HAO-JAN

True-Taoist, good friend Mêng,

Your madness known to one and all,

Young you laughed at rank and power.

Now you sleep in pine-tree clouds.

On moonlit nights floored by the Dragon.

In magic blossom deaf to the World.

You rise above - a hill so high.

I drink the fragrance from afar.

Note: Mêng Hao-jan (689-740AD) lived in the mountains where he studied the Classics and wrote poetry. He tried for the Civil Service but failed the examination. He was a friend of Wang Wei and Li Po. He was careless of worldly achievement and often arrived too drunk to work. The Dragon here is used to mean drink and Imperial disdain, while the blossom is the fragrance of the Tao.

HO CHIH-CHANG

When we met the first time at Ch'ang-an
He called me the 'Lost Immortal'.
Then he loved the Way of Forgetting.
Now under the pine-trees he is dust.
His golden keepsake bought us wine.
Remembering, the tears run down my cheeks.

Note: Ho was a friend and Court official who retired to become a Taoist monk. The Lost Immortals banished from heaven for misbehaviour appeared on earth as extraordinary individuals.

THREE POEMS ON WINE

I

Among the flowers a drink of wine.
I sit alone without a friend.
So I invite the moon,
Then see my shadow, make us three.
The moon can't know how to drink,
Since just my shadow drinks with me.
The moon brought shadow along
To keep me silent company.
Joy should reflect the season.
I sing. That makes the Moon reel.
Get up. Make my shadow sway.
While I'm here let's celebrate.
When I'm drunk each seek the Way,
Tie ourselves to Eternal Journeys,
Swear to meet again in the Milky Way.

II

If the heavens were not in love with wine,
There'd be no Wine Star in the sky.
And if earth wasn't always drinking,
There'd be nowhere called Wine Spring.
I've heard that pure wine makes the Sage.
Even the cloudy makes us wise.
If even the wise get there through drink,
What's the point of True Religions?
Three times and I understand the Way,
Six and I'm one again with Nature.
Only the things we know when we're drunk
Can never be expressed when we're sober.

III

Third month in Ch'ang-an city,
Knee-deep in a thousand fallen flowers.
Alone in Spring who can stand this sadness?
Or sober see transient things like these?
Long life or short, rich or poor,
Our destiny's determined by the world.
But drinking makes us one with life and death,
The Myriad Things we can barely fathom.
Drunk, Heaven and Earth are gone.
Stilled, I clutch my lonely pillow.
Forgetting that the Self exists,
That is the mind's greatest joy.

LAMENT FOR MR TAI

Wine-maker there by Yellow Fountains,

'Eternal Spring' that's still your vintage.

Without Li Po on Night's Terrace

Who can there be to bring you custom?

Note: The Huangquan, the Yellow Fountains, and Night's Terrace, are names for the gloomy realm of the dead below the earth inhabited by spiritual and ethereal beings.

WAKING FROM DRUNKEN SLEEP ON A SPRING DAY.

Life is a dream. No need to stir.
Remembering this I'm drunk all day.
Lying helpless beside the porch,
Waking to see the deep garden.
One bird calls among the flowers.
Ask myself what's the season?
Song of the oriole in Spring breezes,
Voice of beauty sadly moves me.
Is there wine? Ah, fill the cup.
Sing and watch the white moon rise,
until song's end and sense is gone.

DRINKING IN THE MOUNTAINS.

Mountain flowers open in our faces.

You and I are triply lost in wine.

I'm drunk, my friend, sleepy. Rise and go.

With your dawn lute, return, if you wish, and stay.

OLD POEM

Did Chuang Chou dream he was the butterfly?
Or the butterfly dream he was Chuang Chou?
In the single body's transformations
See the vortex of the Myriad Creatures.
No mystery then that the Magic Seas
Shrank again to crystal streams,
Or down by Ch'ang-an's Green Gate
The gardener was Marquis of Tung-Ling.
If this is the fate of fame and power,
What is it for - this endless striving?

Note: The Myriad Creatures are the manifestations of the Tao, as distinct from the Tao itself. The Mythical Islands of the Immortals in the East were located in the Magic Seas, which in a legend were said to be dwindling to nothing. When the Han Dynasty overthrew the Ch'in, The Marquis of Tung-Ling was reduced to growing melons by the Green Gate, one of the eastern gates of the capital, Ch'ang-an.

THE RIVER-CAPTAIN'S WIFE – A LETTER

I with my hair in its first fringe
Romped outside breaking flower-heads.
You galloped by on bamboo horses.
We juggled green plums round the well.
Living in Chang-kan village,
Two small people without guile.

At fourteen I married you sir,
So bashful I could only hide,
My frowning face turned to the wall.
Called after - never looking back.

Fifteen before I learnt to smile.
Yearned to be one with you forever.
You to be the Ever-Faithful.
I to not sit lonely, waiting.

At sixteen you sir went away,
Through White King's Gorge, by Yen Rock's rapids,
When the Yangtze's at its highest,
Where the gibbons cried above you.

Here by the door your last footprints,
Slowly growing green mosses,
So deep I cannot sweep them,
Leaves so thick from winds of autumn.

September's yellow butterflies
Twine together in our west garden.
What I feel – it hurts the heart.
Sadness makes my beauty vanish.

When you come down from far places,
Please will you write me a letter?
As far as the farthest reaches,
I'll come out to welcome you.

THE EXILE'S LETTER

(To Yüan)

Remember how Tung built us a place to drink in
At Lo-yang south of the T'ien-ching bridge?
White jade and gold bought songs and laughter.
We drank forgetting Court and princes.
Those amongst us, wisest and bravest
On all this side of rivers and oceans,
Hearts high as clouds, and you and I together,
Cared nothing at crossing lakes and mountains
Only to share our thoughts and feelings.

Then I went out south-east to cut the laurel,
You north of Lo River still lost in dreams.
No joy in being parted. Soon back again in mountains,
Tracking the thirty-six twists and turns of valley,
By the streams bright with a thousand flowers,
By endless waters,
Hearing pine-trees sighing,
Till we met the Hang-tung Governor
On a gold and silver saddle,
And Hu the True-Taoist drew us with his pipe playing,
Making unearthly music out of the high tower,
Strange sounds of the mating phoenix.
The Governor's sleeves kept time to the music,
So that he rose, drunk, and danced a little,
Brought his brocade coat, covered my body.
I fell asleep, head resting in his lap.

By day our hearts rose to the nine heavens.
At evening we scattered like blown stars or rain,
I to my far mountain over hills and waters,
You to your own house by the bridge of Wei.

That winter I made your father's North City,
Loved you for the way you did me honour,
Sharing your wealth, thinking nothing of it.
Wine there - in cups of amber,
Food there - on plates of jade.
I ate and drank, no thoughts of returning.
We went out to the west. The river parts there,
Round the ancient shrine of a Prince of Chou.
Boats on the waters to drums and piping.
Waves made of dragon scales. Jade-green rushes.
We drank and drank, lived the passing moments,
Forgetting how they go like blossoms or snowfall.
Flushed with wine, warm in glow of sunset,
The hundred-foot deep pool mirroring bright faces,
Dancing-girls delicate as willows in the moonlight,
Notes lost in the silken sleeves' fluttering.
A white breeze blew their song to the sky,
Winding through the air, twisting in the cloud-lanes.
Never again. Never again such joy.

I went west but got no promotion.
White-headed back to eastern hills.
Met once more south of Wei's bridge.
Parted again north of Tso's terrace.
And if you ask my feelings at parting,
They were inside me like Spring flowers falling.

No way to say what's in the heart. Never.
I call in the boy. Have him kneel here, tie this,
To send my feelings through a thousand miles.

JADE STAIRS GRIEVANCE

On jade stairs the white of dewfall.

Deeply soaked the silken slippers.

She lets fall the crystal blind.

Sees, through gauze, a Moon of Autumn.

Note: She is a concubine in the Imperial Palace to which the jade stairs lead, but the white dewdrops on jade are also the tears on her face, the absent 'dew' of sexual union, and the half-month White Dew in the autumn lunar calendar. The soaked slippers indicate she has been there for hours, neglected and self-neglecting. The crystal blind is a jewelled curtain, but also eyelashes wet with tears. She is no longer young, herself a chilled autumn moon. The grievance is unspoken, but implicit.

YEARNING

Misted the flowers weep as light dies
Moon of white silk sleeplessly cries.
Stilled - Phoenix wings.
Touched - Mandarin strings.

This song tells secrets that no one knows
To far Yenjan on Spring breeze it goes.
To you it flies
Through the night skies.

Sidelong - Eyes. How
White tears fill now!
Heart's pain? Come see -
In this mirror with me.

Note: She is a professional courtesan speaking to the absent man with whom fatally she has fallen in love. She has exchanged the Phoenix zither for the Mandarin Duck zither (decorated as such?) that is she has exchanged sensual feelings symbolised by the Phoenix for those of conjugal affection symbolised by the Mandarin ducks. The sidelong glance was the way a dancing girl might attract a man's attention. The Yang sunlight has faded. Yin mist, petals, damp silk and white moon bringing dew are emblems of her tears.

THE ROOSTING CROWS

On Soochow's terrace the crows find their nests.
The King of Wu in his palace drinks with Hsi Shih.
Songs of Wu, Dances of Chu quicken their pleasure,
One half of the sun is caught in the valley's throat.

The clock's silver arrow marks the passing hours.
They rise early to see the autumn moon,
Watch it sink down into deep river.
Daylight glows in the East. Dawn renews their joy.

Note: King Wu and his consort the legendary beauty Hsi Shih provide an analogy for Hsüan Tsung and Yang Kuei-fei. The crow is a Yang symbol associated with the sun.

LU MOUNTAIN, KIANGSI

I climbed west on Incense Cloud Peak.
South I saw the spray-filled falls
Dropping for ten thousand feet
Sounding in a hundred gorges,
Suddenly as if lightning shone,
Strange as if light-wet rainbows lifted.
I thought the Milky Way had shattered,
Scattering stars through the clouds, downwards.

Looking up an even greater force.
Nature's powers are so intense.
The Cosmic Wind blows there without stop.
The river's moon echoes back the light
Into vortices where waters rush.
On both sides the clear walls were washed,
By streams of pearl broken into mist,
By clouds of foam whitening over rock.

Let me reach those Sublime Hills
Where peace comes to the quiet heart.
No more need to find the magic cup.
I'll wash the dust, there, from my face,
And live in those regions that I love,
Separated from the Human World.

Note: Lu Mountain is a Taoist sacred site in Kiangsi Province.

TO MY WIFE ON LU-SHAN MOUNTAIN

Visiting the nun Rise-In-Air,

You must be near her place in those blue hills.

The river's force helps pound the mica,

The wind washes rose bay tree flowers.

If you find you can't leave that refuge,

Invite me there to see the sunset's fire.

Note: Pounded mica and rose bay were both used as Taoist medicines.

REACHING THE HERMITAGE

At evening I make it down the mountain.

Keeping company with the moon.

Looking back I see the paths I've taken

Blue now, blue beneath the skyline.

You greet me, show the hidden track,

Where children pull back hawthorn curtains,

Reveal green bamboo, the secret path,

Vines that touch the traveller's clothes.

I love finding space to rest,

Clear wine to enjoy with you.

Wind in the pines till voices stop,

Songs till the Ocean of Heaven pales.

I get drunk and you are happy,

Both of us pleased to forget the world.

Note: Meeting an adept at a Taoist hermitage, Li thinks about the state of his own dislocated life compared with the hidden, childish, unassuming, but intoxicating nature of the Tao.

HARD JOURNEY

Gold painted jars - wines worth a thousand.

Jade carved dishes - food costing more.

I throw the chopsticks down,

Food and wine are tasteless.

Draw my magic sword,

Mind confused stare round me.

See the ice floes block the Yellow River.

Feel the snowfall shroud the T'ai-hang Mountains.

Quiet again I cast in dark waters,

Find the fragile boat that might drift sunwards.

Hard Journey. So many side-tracks.

Turn after turn, and where am I?

New breezes flatten down the waves ahead.

I'll set cloud sails, cross the Blue Horizon.

Li Po (699-762 AD)

'WE FOUGHT FOR - SOUTH OF THE WALLS
DIED FOR - NORTH OF THE RAMPARTS' (TO AN OLD TUNE)

We fought for Mulberry Springs

Die now for Garlic River.

Wash our swords in Parthian Seas,

Feed our mounts on T'ien Shan snows.

Thousands of miles to and fro.

The Three Armies tired and old.

These Huns kill instead of ploughing,

Sow white bones in desert sand.

Ch'in built the Great Wall.

Han keeps the bright beacons.

These fires never die.

These wars never end.

Hand to hand we fight and fail,

Horses screaming to the skies.

Kites and crows pick at our flesh

Perch on dead trees with our dead.

We paint the grasses red,

Because our General had a plan.

The sword I say's an evil thing.

A wise man keeps it from his hand.

Note: The Mulberry and Garlic Rivers are north and west beyond the Great Wall (as in the old song they represent short-term and ultimately worthless objectives). The 'Parthian Seas' denote the far West and Turkestan, say Parthia and Central Asia of Han times, from the Persian Gulf to the Caspian and Aral Seas. The T'ien Shan are the 'Celestial Mountains' dividing China from Turkestan. The Huns are the Hsiung-nu of Central Asia. The T'ang armies were defeated in northern Turkestan at the battle of the Taras River in 751AD. The last lines are a paraphrase of lines from the Tao Te Ching (Book I, XXXI).

REMEMBERING THE SPRINGS AT CH'IH-CHOU

Peach-tree flowers over rising waters.

White drowned stones, then free again.

Wistaria-blossom on quivering branches.

Clear blue sky. The waxing moon.

How many tight-coiled scrolls of bracken,

On green tracks where I once walked?

When I'm back from exile in Yeh-lang,

There I'll transmute my bones to gold.

Note: Li was banished to Yeh-lang in Yunnan in the extreme south-west, though pardoned under an amnesty before he reached it. He passed the springs at Ch'ih-chou on his slow journey towards it up the Yangtze.

➤ TU FU (712-770 AD) ➤

Winter Landscape, Li Shan（12th century）

NIGHT JOURNEY THOUGHTS

Bent grasses in slender breeze.
Boat's mast high in empty night.
Starlight shining near the plain.
Moon floating on river's light.
All this writing, but no name.
Illness and years, without a place.
Drifting, wandering, what am I?
A white bird over earth and sky.

Spring in Ch'ang-an

Fallen States still have hills and streams.

Cities, in Spring, have leaves and grass.

Though tears well at half-open flowers.

Though parted birds rise with secret fears.

War beacons shine through triple moons.

Home news is worth more than gold.

Grey hairs, tugged at every disaster,

Thin on this head that's too small for its cap.

MOON AT NIGHT IN CH'ANG-AN

North of here in the moonlight
She too looks up in loneliness.
I am sad for our little children,
Too young to think of far off Ch'ang-an.

Clouds of hair wet with jewelled mist.
Cold light on arms of jade.
When will we two stir the silk curtains
While one moon shows the stain of tears?

Note: Tu is in the occupied capital. The past glory is already distant in time. His wife and children are in Fu-chou in the north-east. Those who are parted are linked to each other through watching the same moon.

BY THE WATERS OF WEI

Grieving silently and ageing,

Going secretly by Spring waters,

By closed palaces along the river.

New reeds, fresh willows, green for no one.

Rainbow Banners passed hibiscus flowers,

Once, between South Gardens shining faces,

First Lady of the Han, Flying Swallow,

Sitting by her Lord in his carriage.

Maids of Honour with their bows and arrows

Mounted on white horses with gold bridles,

Glanced and shot their careless shafts together,

Killing with a single gleam of laughter.

Bright eyes. Clear smile. Where is She now?

Spirits of the blood-defiled are homeless.

Beyond the Wei's east-running waters

One entered silence, One was left behind.

Pity's tears remember vanished hours

By waters and by flowers still the same.

Now curfew, and the dust of Tartar horsemen.

I'll head north to reach the south again.

Note: The ill-fated Yang Kuei-fei, whom Hsüan Tsung grieved for so deeply is, by analogy, Flying Swallow consort of the Han Emperor Ch'êng. Tu is probably slipping away to join Su-tsung the Emperor in the North hoping that way to return one day to Ch'ang-an's light-filled South Gardens.

BALLAD OF THE WAR WAGONS

Noise of wagons. Cry of Horses.
Every man carries weapons.
Wives and children run beside them,
Mothers, fathers, gazing after,
Till the bridgehead's drowned in dust.

Tug at cloth sleeves, clutch and weep.
Wailing lifts to dark clouds.
When the watcher questions why,
Answer comes, 'We are the levy'.
At fifteen guard the Yellow River,
At forty work to feed the army.
Young the headman tied your headscarf.
Old you're destined for the borders,
Where the blood is spilt like rainfall,
Where the Han still ask for more.

To the east two hundred places
Where a thousand farms lie fallow.
Though strong women pull the plough now
East and west are vanished furrows,
We who fight the toughest battles
Driven on like dogs or cattle.
We have learned that sons are bad news,
Better only to have daughters,
Who can marry, where their home is,
When a son is dead and rotten.

By Kokonor along the shoreline,
Whitened bones that no one buries,
New ghosts wail with those before them,
Dark clouds gather to their howling.

THE HOMECOMING (FROM THE JOURNEY NORTH)

Slowly we went on country roads,
Smoke blew rarely on the breeze,
Meeting some who'd suffered wounds,
Weeping blood, they cried out loud.
When I looked back to Feng-hsiang
Saw the banners in pale light,
Climbing upwards in cold hills,
Found where men and horses drank.
Till below us Pin-chou Plains,
Parted by the Ching's fierce torrent,
Where the Wild Tigers stood,
And split the rocks when they roared.

Wild flowers in dull autumn,
Beside stones smashed by wagons,
Made my heart reach the clouds.
Simple things give us joy.
Mountain berries, glittering jewels
Hidden in the densest tangle,
Scarlet like the cinnabar sands,
Black as if splashed with lacquer,
Washed by the rain and dew,
Sour and sweet the fruits of nature,
Bring to mind Peach Blossom Story,
Not this life that's gone and wasted.

Downhill at last far-off Fu-chou,

Scrambling through the rocky clefts,

Down towards the river's edge,

Leave the others far behind.

Fieldmice, little guardians, upright,

Listen for the owls in mulberry,

Like Men of Ch'in before the battle.

Moonlight shines here on white bones.

Once a million men positioned

Here to hold the Pass. How many

Ever returned? There perished

Half of Ch'in, now wandering spirits.

I too drowned in alien dust. Back again now.

A year on with whitened hair,

To a poor and simple house,

My dear wife dressed in rags,

Who seeing me cries like rain,

Or fountains bubbling underground.

Here's my son, pride of my days,

With face paler than Spring snow,

Who seeing me turns and weeps,

His dusty feet lacking shoes.

My little daughters by the couch

Patched dresses barely to their knees,

Sea-wave hems that fail to meet,

Sewn with old embroidery -

Nine-faced Tiger, Phoenix wings,

Tacked on haphazardly.

I say ' I'm still not myself.
I'm sick. Must sleep for a while.
But there's something in my bag
To keep you from the winter's cold.

Thick quilts tightly packed -
Inside them there's some paint and powder.'
My wife's thin face is beautified,
The girls, chattering, dress her hair,

Copying their happy mother,
Colouring their clever fingers
Till the scarlet rouge makes eyebrows
For two pretty little demons.

Alive! With my children! Home!
Forgetting hunger, worry, pain.
All these questions fired at me,
Who could have the heart to stop them?

Thinking what I've left behind me,
How the noise of love is sweet!

Note: Written in 757AD when Tu left the Imperial camp at Feng-hsiang having occupied a position as a junior official. It was not a great success probably not through any lack of ability on his part, but more likely due to his uncompromising displays of principle and moral courage. He got home to his family whom he had not seen since the capital had been occupied the previous year.

A VISITOR

Southwards, northwards, the Spring waters.
Only flocks of gulls fly in each day.
The flowered path's not yet swept for guests.
The willow gate has opened first for you.
It's simple food we're so far from the City.
In this poor house there's only stale rice-wine.
If you're willing, I can call across the hedge.
Drink it with an Old Neighbour of mine.

FOR GENERAL HUA

All day long in Ch'êng-tu,

Lute-strings, reed-pipes make music.

Half of it lost - in the clouds,

Half of it lost - in the water.

But a song like this one

Is meant for the highest skies.

How often can

An ordinary mortal hear it?

Note: Ch'êng-tu (Brocade City) was the ancient capital of Shu in the South West. The poem was a hint to the young general Hua that he should not let his military success tempt him to aspire to or rebel against the Celestial Throne.

FOR WEI PA

All our days rarely meeting
Like those stars in their constellations,
This evening, what an evening,
We've shared the flickering candle.
Youth and power swiftly pass,
Hair on our heads is quickly white,
Half of those we knew have vanished,
Pain of that knowledge hurts us.
Who'd guess at twenty years,
Before your house saw my return?
Last time you'd not even married.
Now suddenly sons and daughters
Come to cheerfully greet their father's friend.
Start to ask where I come from.
But the conversation's halted
You send them off to fetch the wine-jar,
And pull spring onions in the rain,
Cook them now with yellow millet.
Saying 'Well, we so rarely meet'
Fill my wine-cup ten times over,
Ten but still I'm not quite tipsy,
Filled with feelings of deep friendship.
Tomorrow the high mountains part us,
Lost again in the world.

TU FU TO T'AO CHIEN - ACROSS THE CENTURIES

Gone in a flash the bright flowers.
Old. How I wish they would stay!
Why can't these present things
Be back in our younger days?
Drinking - sets free the mind.
Writing - unfolds the heart.
We would meet, T'ao, in this thought,
Though we cannot meet in Time.

TO LI PO

When Death divides us grief is smothered.

Parted by Life it's endless sighs.

South of the River this land's poison.

From you in exile no word comes.

Note: In happier times Tu wrote 'Li, The Most Brilliant, has left the Court so that he is free to chase the Mysteries. Like me he wanders from Liang to Sung. We go to gather magic herbs.'

Tu Fu (712-770 AD)

HIGH AND DRY ON THE YANGTZE

Cutting winds. Clouds high.
Gorge on gorge. Gibbons cry.
Over river-island's sand
white birds swoop and land.
Everywhere leaf fall,
Dry leaves rustling.
Everywhere dark waves,
Endless rippling.
Mile on mile of autumn light
is like this journey.
Climb alone and ill
To the bright balcony.

Life's regrets and failures,
Frost on my forehead.
No longer have a body
To take me where the wine led.

YANGTZE

After night rain, autumn sky.

On bright waves the glow of stars.

Heaven's Ocean white forever.

Yangtze's waves a moment lucent.

Broken necklace. Mirror pearls.

In the sky the Perfect Glass.

Twilight pale on dripping clock,

Dim as dew weighs down the flowers.

Tu Fu (712-770 AD)

DEEP WINTER

Only as skies unfold, the 'Flower in the Leaves'.

Between river and stream the 'Roots of Clouds'.

Cast as shadows, dawn's red boulders:

Cold scars show the past floods.

Yang Chu, simple to share your tears.

Ch'ü Yüan, hard to recall your spirit.

Waves blow in the evening winds.

Where will I rest, and in whose house?

Note: Tu Fu is near the Hisang River south of Lake T'ung-ting and the Yangtze. The sun in the clouds is the 'Flower in the Leaves', the Yang energy that will eventually bring the Spring. The sun, the season, the 'river' of the Empire, and the 'stream' of the self, Tu Fu, are all subject to the rhythms of time and the Tao. The sun is a red boulder in the sky and the 'Roots of Clouds', the red boulders of the Hsiang River, are the shadows of the red morning clouds in the water that were breathed out by the rocks. The red rocks of the present are the clouds of a morning that has passed. The marks on their sides are the visible records of vanished floods. Tu Fu is driven by reality but haunted by the past, its youthful dawn, and its subsequent tears. Yang Chu wept at the crossroads because any road he chose would lead to new crossroads, and could never lead back. Ch'ü Yüan was China's first great (shamanist and Taoist) poet and incorruptible minister of the kingdom of Ch'u, near Lake T'ung-t'ing, who chose to drown in the Mi-lo River, in protest and despair, after being slandered, rejected and banished. His noble suicide is commemorated in the Dragon Boat Festival. Tu Fu identifies with both men.

MEETING LI KUEI-NIEN SOUTH OF THE RIVER

Frequently meeting in Palace of Ch'i.
Hearing you sing in Mansion of Chiu.
So lovely here, South of the River,
Meeting again where petals fall.

Note: Perhaps Tu's last poem, written in the autumn of 770. A famous musician, Li Kuei-nien had performed at Prince Chi's palace and Ts'ui Chiu's mansion, places of the ruined Empire.

PO CHÜ-YI (772-846 AD)

Mountains in Clouds, He Cheng (ca. 1380 – 1470)

THE SONG OF EVERLASTING SORROW

China's Emperor yearning, for beauty that shakes a kingdom,
Reigned for many years, searching but not finding,
Until a child of the Yang, hardly yet grown,
Raised in the inner chamber, unseen by anybody,
But with heavenly graces that could not be hidden,
Was chosen one day for the Imperial household.
If she turned her head and smiled she cast a deep spell,
Beauties of Six Palaces vanished into nothing.
Hair's cloud, pale skin, shimmer of gold moving,
Flowered curtains protected on cool spring evenings.
Those nights were too short. That sun too quick in rising.

The emperor neglected the world from that moment,
Lavished his time on her in endless enjoyment.
She was his springtime mistress, and his midnight tyrant.
Though there were three thousand ladies all of great beauty,
All his gifts were devoted to one person.

Li Palace rose high in the clouds.
The winds carried soft magic notes,
Songs and graceful dances, string and pipe music.
He could never stop himself from gazing at her.

But the Earth reels. War drums fill East Pass,
Drown out 'The Feathered Coat and Rainbow Skirt'.
Great Swallow Pagoda and Hall of Light,
Are bathed in dust - the army fleeing Southwards.
Out there Imperial banners, wavering, pausing
Until by the river forty miles from West Gate,
The army stopped. No one would go forward,
Until horses' hooves trampled willow eyebrows.
Flower on a hairpin. No one to save it.
Gold and jade phoenix. No one retrieved it.
Covering his face the Emperor rode on.
Turned to look back at that place of tears,
Hidden by a yellow dust whirled by a cold wind.

As Shu waters flow green, Shu mountains show blue,
His majesty's love remained, deeper than the new.
White moon of loneliness, cold moon of exile.
Bell-chimes in evening rain were bronze-edged heartbeats.
So when the dragon-car turned again northwards
The Emperor clung to Ma-Wei's dust, never desiring
To leave that place of memories and heartbreak.
Where is the white jade in heaven and earth's turning?

Lakes and gardens are still as they have been,
T'ai-yi's hibiscus, Wei-yang's willows.
A flower-petal was her face, a willow-leaf her eyebrow,
How could it not be grief just to see them?
Plum and pear blossoms blown on spring winds
Maple trees ruined in rains of autumn.
Palaces neglected, filled with weeds and grasses,
Mounds of red leaves spilled on unswept stairways.

Burning the midnight light he could not sleep,
Bells and drums tolled the dark hours,
The Ocean of Heaven bright before dawn,
The porcelain mandarin birds frosted white,
The chill covers of kingfisher blue,
Colder and emptier, year by year.
And the loved spirit never returning.

A Taoist priest of Ling-chun rode the paths of Heaven,
He with his powerful mind knew how to reach the Spirits.
The Courtiers troubled by the Emperor's grieving,
Asked the Taoist priest if he might find her.
He opened the sky-routes, swept the air like lightning,
Looked everywhere, on earth and in heaven,
Scoured the Great Void, and the Yellow Fountains,
But failed in either to find the one he searched for.
Then he heard tales of a magic island
In the Eastern Seas, enchanted, eternal,
High towers and houses in air of five colours,
Perfect Immortals walking between them,
Among them one they called The Ever Faithful,
With her face, of flowers and of snow.

She left her dreams, rose from her pillow,
Opened mica blind and crystal screen,
Hastening, unfastened, clouded hair hanging,
Her light cap unpinned, ran along the pavement.
A breeze in her gauze, flowing with her movement,
As if she danced 'Feathered Coat and Rainbow Skirt'.
So delicate her jade face, drowned with tears of sadness,
Like a spray of pear flowers, veiled with springtime rain.

She asked him to thank her Love, her eyes gleaming,
He whose form and voice she lost at parting.
Her joy had ended in Courts of the Bright Sun,
Moons and dawns were long in Faerie Palace.
When she turned her face to look back earthwards
And see Ch'ang-an - only mist and dust-clouds.
So she found the messenger her lover's gifts
With deep feeling gave him lacquer box, gold hairpin,
Keeping one half of the box, one part of the hairpin,
Breaking the lacquer, splitting the gold.

'Our spirits belong together, like these precious fragments,
Sometime, in earth or heaven, we shall meet again.'
And she sent these words, by the Taoist, to remind him
of their midnight vow, secret between them.
'On that Seventh night, of the Herdboy and the Weaver,
In the silent Palace we declared our dream was
To fly together in the sky, two birds on the same wing,
To grow together on the earth, two branches of one tree.'

Earth fades, Heaven fades, at the end of days.
But Everlasting Sorrow endures always.

Notes: The Emperor is Hsüan Tsung, that is Ming Huang the Glorious Monarch. She is Yang Yü-huan, the Favourite Concubine Yang Kuei-fei.

The war drums are those of the An Lu-shan rebellion that destroyed the greatest period of the Tang Dynasty. The East Pass is the Tung Kuan, loss of which was disastrous to Ch'ang-an since it was the last defensible barrier to the east of the capital. The Da Yen Ta, the Great Swallow Pagoda, still stands on the site of Ch'ang-an, modern Xian. Ma-Wei is the posting station on the Wei River, west of the city, where Yang Kuei-fei was executed to satisfy the demands of the army.

Mandarin birds and kingfisher covers are symbols of conjugal affection. The Herdboy and the Weaver girl, in legend, are the stars Altair in the constellation Aquila (the Eagle) and Vega in the constellation Lyra (the Lyre). (Stars which with Deneb, in Cygnus the Swan, form the northern Summer Triangle). They are lovers separated by the Milky Way. She is allowed to visit him once a year on the seventh night of the seventh month, the first month of autumn, when she passes across the heavens as a meteor, or crosses to him on a bridge of birds. On this night also The Lady of the West descended from the sky to teach the Emperor Wu the secret of immortality.

➤ ALPHABETICAL LIST OF EQUIVALENT ✧ CHINESE NAMES AND TERMS

Names and *terms* in the modern Pinyin system of Romanization are shown last on each line, and the modern Province is shown in brackets after Pinyin location names.

Anhwei Province, Anhui

An Lu-shan (General), An Lushan

Ch'an Buddhism, Qān Buddhism

Ch'ang-an, Chang'an, Sian, Sian-fu, Xi'an (Shaanxi)

Ch'ang-kan (village), Chinkiang, Zhenjiang (Jiangsu)

Ch'ang-sha, Changsha (Hunan)

Chang Yen-yüan, Zhang Yanyuan

Chên-ting, Chenting, Zhengding (Hebei)

Chêng-tu, Ch'eng-tu, Cheng-tu, Chengdu (Sichuan)

Ch'i (spirit, breath, force etc), Qi

Ch'i-chou, Chichow, Kweichih, Guichi (Anhui)

Chiang-ling, Kiangchow, Kiangling, Jiangling (Hubei)

Ch'in Dynasty (221-206BC), Chin Dynasty, Qin Dynasty

Chin-shih (examination), Jinshi

Ching River, King River, Jing (Shaanxi)

Ching Hao, Jing Hao

Chou Dynasty (c. 1122-221BC), Zhou Dynasty

Ch'u Kingdom (Fourth/third century BC), Chu Kingdom

Ch'ü Yüan (poet), Qu Yuan

Chuang-tzu (Taoist), Zhuang Zi, Zhuang Zhou

C'hu-t'ang Gorge (Yangtze), Qutang Xia

Confucius, K'ung-Fu-tzu, Kongfuzi

Feng-hsien, Feng-hsiang, Fengsiang, Fufeng (Shaanxi)

Fu-chou, Fuchow, Fu Xian (Shaanxi)

Han Dynasty (206BC-220AD), Han Dynasty

Han River, Han Kiang, Han Shui

Hankow, Wuhan (Hubei)

Han-yang, Hanyang (Hubei)

Honan Province, Henan

Hopei Province, Hupeh, Hebei

Hsi K'ang, Xi Kang

Hsiang River, Siang Kiang

Hsien (Immortal, sennin), Xian

Hsiung-nu ('Huns'), Xiongnu

Hui-neng, Huineng

Hsüan-tsang (Buddhist Pilgrim), Xuan Zang, Xuanzang

Hsüan-tsung (Emperor, Ming-huang), Xuanzong

Hui-neng (Sixth Ch'an Patriarch), Huineng

Jao-chou, Jaochow, Poyang, Boyang (Jianxi)

Jen (benevolence, goodness), Ren

Kai-feng, Kaifeng (Henan)

Kansu Province, Gansu

Kashgar, Kaxgar, Kashi (Xinjiang)

Khotan, Ho-t'ien, Hotan (Xinjiang)

Kialing River, Kialin Kiang, Jialing Jiang (Sichuan)

Kiangsu Province, Jiangsu

Kiukiang, Jiujiang (Jiangxi)

Kokonor Lake, Koko Nor, Ching Hai, Quinghai Hu (Qinghai)

K'uei-chou, Kweichow, Fengkieh, Fengjie (Sichuan)

Kuo Hsi, Guo Xi

Lant'ien, Lantien, Lantian (Shaanxi)

Lao-tzu, Lao-tze, Laozi

Li Lin-fu (Minister), Li Linfu

Li Po, Li Bai

Liang-yüan, Kweiteh, Shang-kiu, Shangqiu (Henan)

Lo River, Luo He (Henan)

Lop Nor, Lop Nur (Xinjiang)

Loyang, Lo-yang, Luoyang (Henan)

Lu Chi, Lu Ji

Lu-shan, Mount Lu, Lu Shan (Jiangxi)

Lukiang, Lujiang (Anhui)

Mi-lo River, Miluo (Hunan)

Nanking, Nanjing (Jiangsu)

Peking, Pei-ching, Beijing

P'eng-lai (Palace, Islands of the Blessed), Penglai

Pi (jade disc), Bi

Pin-chou, Pinchow, Bin Xian (Shaanxi)

Po Chü-Yi, Po Chü-i, Po Chu-i, Bai Juyi

Poyang, Lake Poyang, Poyang Hu (Jiangxi)

Shang-lin Park, Shanglin

Shansi Province, Shanxi

Shantung Province, Shan-tung, Shandong

Shensi Province, Shaanxi

Shih Chi (The Historical Records), Shi Ji, Shiji

Shih (verse form), Shi

Si Wang Mu (Goddess of the West), Xiwangmu

Soochow, Wuhsien, Suzhou (Shandong)

Ssu-ma Ch'ien (Han Historian 145?-85?BC), Sima Qian

Su-tsung ('Emperor in the North'), Su Tsung, Suzong

Su T'ung-po, Su Shi, Su Dongpo

Suchow, Tungshan, Xuzhou (Jiangsu)

Sung Dynasty (960 North-1279AD Southern),Song Dynasty

Szu-ch'uan Province, Szechwan, Sichuan

T'ai-shan, Mount Tai, Tai Shan (Shandong)

T'ai-yüan, Yangku, Taiyuan (Shanxi)

Taklamakan Desert, Taklimakan Shamo

T'ang Dynasty (618-907AD), Tang Dynasty

Tang-t'u, T'ai-p'ing, Taiping, Tangtu, Dangtu (Anhui)

Tao, Dao: Taoism, Daoism: Tao-Te Ching: Daode Jing

T'ao Ch'ien, T'ao Yüan-ming, Tao Yuanming, Tao Qian

Tarim Basin, Tarim Pendi

T'ien Shan, Tien Shan, Tian Shan (Xinjiang)

Sui Dynasty, Sui Dynasty (581-618AD)

Tu Fu, Du Fu

T'un-huang, Dunhuang (Gansu)

T'ung Kuan Pass, Tungkwan, Tongguan (Shaanxi)

Tung-t'ing Lake,Tung Ting Hu, Dongting Hu (Hunan)

Tzu-jan (spontaneity,naturalness), Ziran

Wang Chao-chün (wife of Tartar Khan), Wang Zhaojun

Wei River, Wei Ho (Shaanxi)

Wu Gorge (Yangtze), Wu Xia (Sichuan)

Wu-ch'ang, Wuchang (Hubei)

Wu-ti Emperor of Han, Han Wudi

Yang Chu, Yang Zhu

Yang Kuei-fei (Yang Yü-huan, Consort), Yang Guifei

Yang Kuo-chung, Yang Guozhong

Yangchow, Yangzhou (Jiangsu)

Yangtze River, Yangtze Kiang, Yangzi Jiang, Chang Jiang

Yeh-lang River, Yehlang, Yalong Jiang (Yunnan)

Yellow River, Hwang-ho, Hwang Ho, Huang He

Yo-chou, Yochow, Yoyang, Yueyang (Hunan)

Yü-chang, Nan-k'ang, Nanchang (Jiangxi)

Yüeh-fu (ballad verse form), yuefu

Yünnan Province, Yunnan

Yumen (old town), Yu-men, Jiayuguan(Gansu)

➤ SIMPLIFIED CHRONOLOGY ❧

CHINA	CHINESE CULTURE	WESTERN EUROPE
Paleolithic **(500,000-5000BC)** - L'antien Man - Peking Man - Homo Sapiens	- Stone Tools	- Cave Paintings (Altamira, Lascaux)
Neolithic **(5000-1000BC)** - Yungshao Culture - Lungshan Culture - Liang-chu Culture	- Metallurgy in Bronze - Pottery, Jade Carvings	- Megaliths, Pottery (Stonehenge, Carnac) - Minoan Culture
Shang Dynasty **(c.1480-1050BC)** - Tomb building - Ritual sacrifice	- Bronze vessels, Writing - Divination (Scapulamancy) - Statuettes	- Bronze Age - Urnfield Culture - Mycenaean Culture
Chou Dynasty **(c.1122-221BC)** - Western Chou - Spring and Autumn Period - Warring States Period	- Book of Songs - Confucius (6th Century) - Lao-Tzu - Mencius	- Iron Age - Hallstatt Culture - La Tène Culture - Phoenicians - Classical Greece - Roman Republic - Alexander the Great
Ch'in Dynasty **(221-206BC)**	- Unified empire - Great Wall - Centralisation - Regularised script - F'eng shui (Geomancy)	- Second Punic War (218-201BC)

Han Dynasty (202BC-220AD)
- Emperor Wu-ti (r.141-87BC)
- Warfare against the Huns
- Silk Road trade with the West
- Ch'ang-an established

- Buddhism 65AD
- Ssu-Ma-Ch'ien (historian) (c.145-c.86BC)

- Defeat of Carthage (146BC)
- Fall of Roman Republic
- Imperial Rome

Period of Division (220-581AD)
- Disunity and internal warfare
Kingdom of Wu (222-280AD)
Kindom of Shu (221-263AD)

T'ao Ch'ien(365-427AD)
- Expansion of Buddhism

- Late Roman Empire
- Early Byzantium
- Attila's invasion
- Barbarian migration

Sui Dynasty (581-618AD)
- Re-unification of the Empire

- Grand Canal, Road system
- Rebuilding of Ch'ang-an

- Mohammed (570-632AD)

T'ang Dynasty (618-907AD)
- Empress Wu (c.627-705AD)
- Hsüan-tsung (685-761AD, r.712-756AD)
- An Lu-shan rebellion 755AD
- Flight of Emperor 756AD
- Loss of Central Asian territory
- Weakened dynasty to 907AD

- Ch'an Buddhism
Wang Wei (699-759AD)
Li Po (701-762AD)
Tu Fu (712-770AD)
Po Chü-Yi (772-846AD)

- Middle Byzantium
- Rise of Islam
- Kgdm. of the Franks
- Langobard Kgdm. in Italy (568-774).
- Jutes,Angles,Saxons invade England.
- Battle of Tours 732 (curbs Islamic expansion)

Five Dynasties and Ten Kingdoms (907-959AD)

**Northern Sung
(960-1126AD)**

- Neo-Confucianism

- The Normans
- Battle of Hastings 1066
- First Crusade

**Southern Sung
(1127-1179AD)**

- Landscape painting

- Second Crusade

➤ Index of Poems by First Line ⤙

⤳ Map of T'ang China ⤳

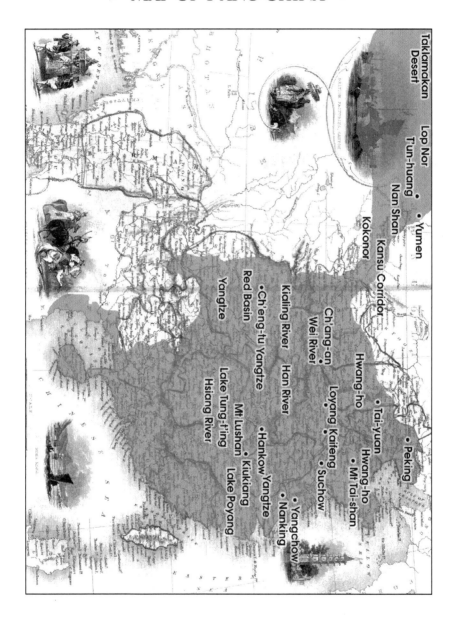

⇗ ABOUT THE AUTHOR ⇖

Anthony Kline lives in England. He graduated in Mathematics from the University of Manchester, and was Chief Information Officer (Systems Director) of a large UK Company, before dedicating himself to his literary work and interests. He was born in 1947. His work consists of translations of poetry; critical works, biographical history with poetry as a central theme; and his own original poetry. He has translated into English from Latin, Ancient Greek, Classical Chinese and the European languages. He also maintains a deep interest in developments in Mathematics and the Sciences.

He continues to write predominantly for the Internet, making all works available in download format, with an added focus on the rapidly developing area of electronic books. His most extensive works are complete translations of Ovid's Metamorphoses and Dante's Divine Comedy.

Made in the USA
Lexington, KY
16 December 2017